ZAGAT®
CELEBRATING 30 YEARS

Los Angeles
Nightlife
Ninth Edition

D1742862

LOCAL EDITOR
Gary Baum
STAFF EDITOR
Bill Corsello

Published and distributed by
Zagat Survey, LLC
4 Columbus Circle
New York, NY 10019
T: 212.977.6000
E: lanightlife@zagat.com
www.zagat.com

ACKNOWLEDGMENTS

We thank Marvin Bae, August Brown, Adam Di Panni, Marty Gadznowski, Jessica Gelt, Tammy Gishri, Krista Jablonski, Alexis Johnson, Jeff Kobayashi, Matt Porter, Kathryn Romeyn, Steven Shukow and Kieumai Vo, as well as the following members of our staff: Aleksandra Shander (editorial assistant), Brian Albert, Sean Beachell, Maryanne Bertollo, Jane Chang, Sandy Cheng, Reni Chin, Larry Cohn, Alison Flick, Jeff Freier, Curt Gathje, Andrew Gelardi, Michelle Golden, Justin Hartung, Karen Hudes, Roy Jacob, Garth Johnston, Ashunta Joseph, Cynthia Kilian, Natalie Lebert, Mike Liao, Christina Livadiotis, Dave Makulec, Andre Pilette, Kimberly Rosado, Becky Ruthenburg, Jacqueline Wasilczyk, Sharon Yates, Anna Zappia and Kyle Zolner.

© 2009 Zagat Survey, LLC
ISBN-13: 978-1-60478-161-8
ISBN-10: 1-60478-161-0
Printed in the
United States of America

CELEBRATING 30 YEARS

ZAGAT SURVEY

Back in 1979, we never imagined that an idea born during a wine-fueled dinner with friends would take us on an adventure that's lasted three decades – and counting.

The idea – that the collective opinions of avid consumers can be more accurate than the judgments of an individual critic – led to a hobby involving friends rating NYC restaurants. And that hobby grew into Zagat Survey, which today has over 350,000 participants worldwide weighing in on everything from airlines, bars, dining and golf to hotels, movies, shopping, tourist attractions and more.

By giving consumers a voice, we – and our surveyors – had unwittingly joined a revolution whose concepts (user-generated content, social networking) were largely unknown 30 years ago. However, those concepts caught fire with the rise of the Internet and have since transformed not only restaurant criticism but also virtually every aspect of the media, and we feel lucky to have been at the start of it all.

As we celebrate Zagat's 30th year, we'd like to thank everyone who has participated in our surveys. We've enjoyed hearing and sharing your frank opinions and look forward to doing so for many years to come. As we always say, our guides and online content are really "yours."

We'd also like to express our gratitude by supporting **Action Against Hunger,** an organization that works to meet the needs of the hungry in over 40 countries. To find out more, visit www.zagat.com/action.

Nina and Tim Zagat

Contents

Ratings & Symbols

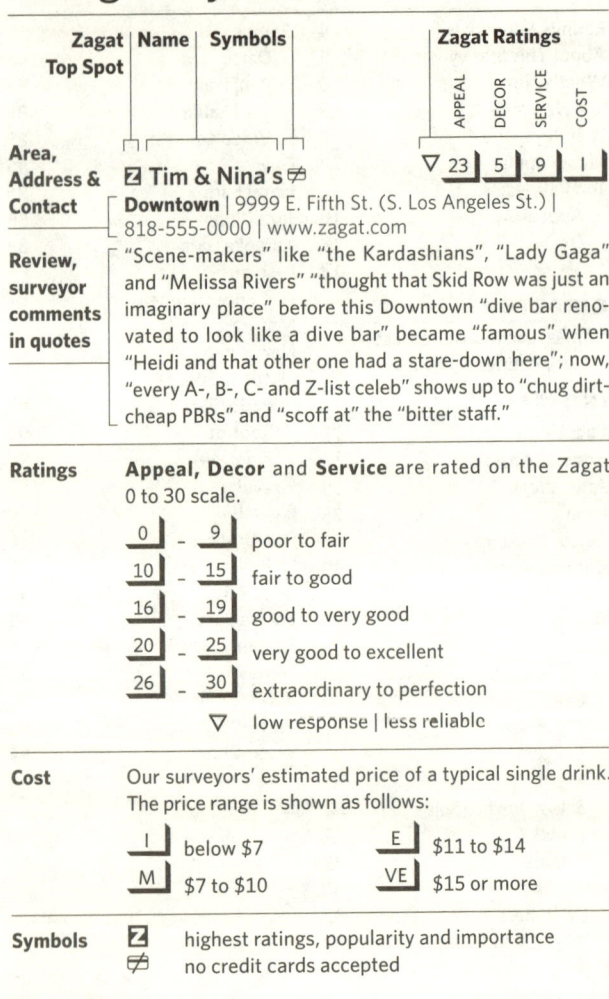

	Zagat Top Spot	Name	Symbols		Zagat Ratings			
					APPEAL	DECOR	SERVICE	COST

Area, Address & Contact

Z Tim & Nina's ⊘

∇ 23 | 5 | 9 | I

Downtown | 9999 E. Fifth St. (S. Los Angeles St.) | 818-555-0000 | www.zagat.com

Review, surveyor comments in quotes

"Scene-makers" like "the Kardashians", "Lady Gaga" and "Melissa Rivers" "thought that Skid Row was just an imaginary place" before this Downtown "dive bar renovated to look like a dive bar" became "famous" when "Heidi and that other one had a stare-down here"; now, "every A-, B-, C- and Z-list celeb" shows up to "chug dirt-cheap PBRs" and "scoff at" the "bitter staff."

Ratings

Appeal, Decor and **Service** are rated on the Zagat 0 to 30 scale.

0	–	9	poor to fair
10	–	15	fair to good
16	–	19	good to very good
20	–	25	very good to excellent
26	–	30	extraordinary to perfection
∇			low response	less reliable

Cost

Our surveyors' estimated price of a typical single drink. The price range is shown as follows:

I below $7   E $11 to $14
M $7 to $10   VE $15 or more

Symbols

Z highest ratings, popularity and importance
⊘ no credit cards accepted

About This Survey

Here are the results of the Ninth Edition of our **Los Angeles Nightlife Survey,** covering 253 bars, clubs and lounges in Los Angeles and the surrounding areas. Like all our guides, this one is based on the collective opinions of thousands of avid consumers – 1,774 all told.

WHO PARTICIPATED: Input from these enthusiasts forms the basis for the ratings and reviews in this guide (their comments are shown in quotation marks within the reviews). They bring an annual total of roughly 167,000 nights' worth of experience to this Survey. We sincerely thank these participants.

OUR EDITOR: Special thanks go to our local editor, Gary Baum, senior editor at *Angeleno* magazine.

ABOUT ZAGAT: This marks our 30th year reporting on the shared experiences of consumers like you. Today we have over 350,000 surveyors and now cover airlines, bars, dining, entertaining, fast food, golf, hotels, movies, music, resorts, shopping, spas, theater and tourist attractions in over 100 countries.

BE A SURVEYOR: We invite you to join any of our surveys at **ZAGAT.com.** There you can share your experiences with thousands of others year-round. In exchange for doing so, you'll receive a free copy of the resulting guide when published.

AVAILABILITY: Zagat guides are available in all major bookstores as well as on **ZAGAT.com.** You can also access our content when on the go via **ZAGAT.mobi** (for web-enabled mobile devices) and **ZAGAT TO GO** (for smartphones). All make it possible to contact thousands of places with just one click.

FEEDBACK: To improve this guide, we invite your comments and suggestions. Just contact us at **lanightlife@zagat.com.**

New York, NY
July 1, 2009

Nina and Tim Zagat

What's New

LA's nightlife scene is taking its fair share of shots in these tough times, but it's far from knocked out, as evidenced by an intriguing slate of premieres. Still, the weakened economy and escalated tabs (the city's per-drink average has risen to $11.66, second only to Las Vegas at $12.24) no doubt help explain why 54% of surveyors say they're going out less often than they did last year. When they do hit the town, they're taking cost-cutting measures such as being more mindful of prices when ordering (33%), choosing less-expensive places (32%) and partaking in fewer rounds (30%).

THE COMEBACK KIDS: Revivals are this year's mini-trend, beginning with Crescent Heights' thoroughly rehabbed **Guy's. Largo** now hits the stage of WeHo's Coronet Theater, **The Conga Room** is newly ensconced in larger digs in Downtown's LA Live and WeHo gay staple **Micky's** has risen from the ashes of a 2007 fire.

DOWNTOWN ASCENSION: Downtown's cred as a night-owl destination continues to rise. Vino vortex **Corkbar** opened near concert venue **Club Nokia** (in LA Live), while subterranean **Crocker Club,** wine-and-beer bar **The Must** and speakeasy simulacra **The Association** and **The Varnish** set down roots in the Historic Core. Rounding out the newcomers are gastropub **The Lab** and hotel lounge **Suede.**

PLANET HOLLYWOOD: Seemingly velvet-roped off from the rest of the belt-tightening universe, Hollywood (voted both the hottest *and* most overrated neighborhood for after-dark revelry) debuted expensive enclaves such as celeb-haven **Bardot,** deco-bedecked **Bar Delux,** eco-conscious **Ecco** and radiant **Halo.** On the west side of the 'hood, **h.wood** resembles a warehouse, while **MyHouse** re-creates a mansion.

WHAT'S YOUR POISON? On weeknights, 35% of surveyors say they prefer wine, 26% fancy mixed drinks and 21% choose beer. On weekends, 67% favor cocktails – however, merely 18% of respondents applaud the idea of master mixology, while 24% deem it a harmless gimmick and 47% suspect it's just an excuse to charge more.

Los Angeles, CA
July 1, 2009

Gary Baum

Menus, photos, voting and more – free at ZAGAT.com

KEY NEWCOMERS

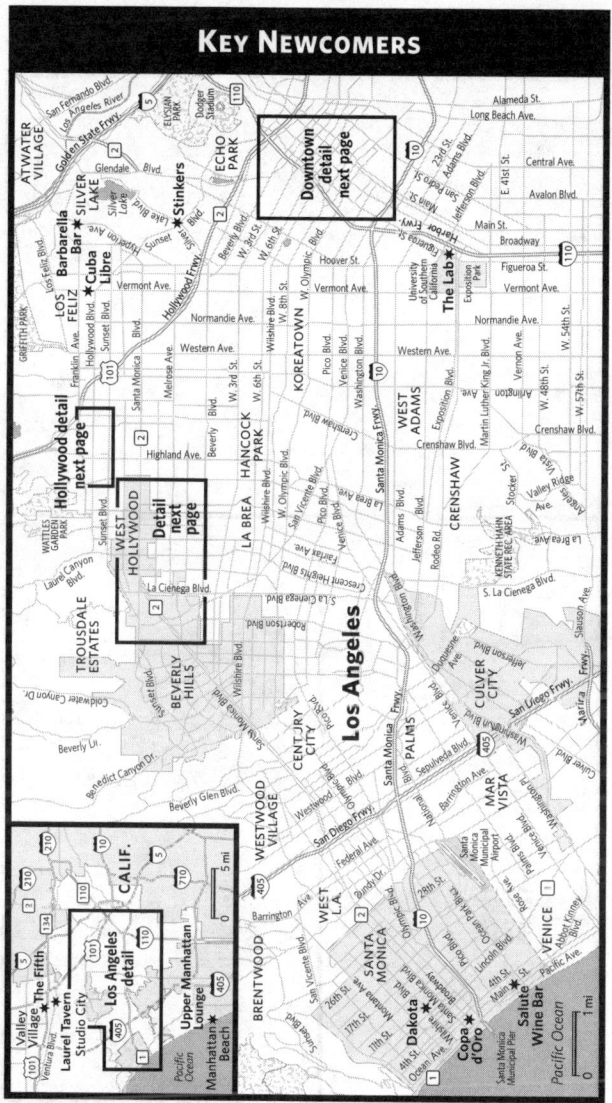

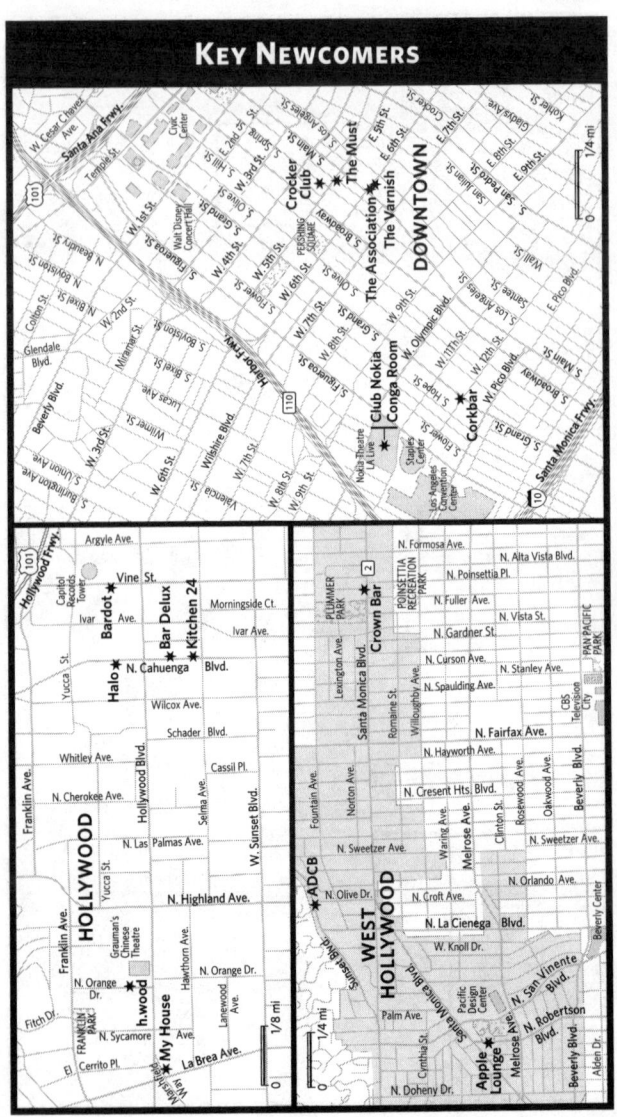

KEY NEWCOMERS

DOWNTOWN

Santa Ana Frwy.
Civic Center
Walt Disney Concert Hall
Crocker Club
The Must
The Association
The Varnish
Club Nokia
Conga Room
Corkbar
Nokia Theatre
LA Live
Staples Center
Los Angeles Convention Center

HOLLYWOOD

Capitol Records Tower
Bardot
Vine St.
Bar Delux
Kitchen 24
Halo
N. Cahuenga Blvd.
Grauman's Chinese Theatre
h.wood
My House

WEST HOLLYWOOD

Crown Bar
PLUMMER PARK
POINSETTIA RECREATION PARK
PAN PACIFIC PARK
CBS Television City
ADCB
Apple Lounge
Pacific Design Center
Beverly Center

Key Newcomers

Our editors' take on the year's top arrivals. See page 88 for a full list.

ADCB

Apple Lounge

Association

Barbarella Bar

Bar Delux

Bardot

Club Nokia

Conga Room

Copa d'Oro

Corkbar

Crocker Club

Crown Bar

Cuba Libre

Dakota

Fifth

Halo

h.wood

Kitchen 24

Lab

Laurel Tavern

Must

MyHouse

Salute Wine Bar

Stinkers

Upper Manhattan

Varnish

Best Buys

In order of Bang for the Buck rating.

1. Intelligentsia
2. Ercole's
3. Bar 107
4. Tom Bergin's
5. Bigfoot Lodge
6. Laurel Tavern
7. McCabe's
8. Coach & Horses
9. Short Stop
10. York
11. Griffin
12. LAMILL
13. Bordello
14. Echo/Echoplex
15. Library Alehouse
16. Spaceland
17. Drawing Room
18. HMS Bounty
19. Cock 'n Bull
20. Casey's Irish

Most Popular

1	Father's Office	**11**	Bar Marmont
2	Asia de Cuba	**12**	Polo Lounge
3	Abbey	**13**	House of Blues
4	Edison Lounge	**14**	Peninsula Bar
5	Standard (Downtown)	**15**	Moonshadows
6	Chateau Marmont	**16**	Bodega Wine
7	Hotel Bel-Air	**17**	Les Deux
8	Barney's Beanery	**18**	Shutters Lobby
9	Skybar	**19**	Avalon Hollywood
10	Mastro's Steak	**20**	Cat & Fiddle

Top Appeal Ratings

Excludes places with low votes, unless indicated by a ▽.

<u>27</u> Hotel Bel-Air
Association
Polo Lounge

<u>26</u> Mastro's Steak
Edison Lounge
Chateau Marmont
Sidebar
Peninsula Bar
Bar Marmont

<u>25</u> Langham Huntington

Shutters Lobby
Tiki-Ti
Hotel Café
Vibrato
Moonshadows
Skybar
Standard (Downtown)
Laurel Tavern

<u>24</u> Seven Grand
Asia de Cuba

BY CATEGORY

AFTER WORK

<u>25</u> Standard (Downtown)
<u>24</u> Seven Grand

Firefly
<u>22</u> Library Bar
Whiskey Blue

BARS

27 Association
26 Sidebar
25 Tiki-Ti
   Laurel Tavern
24 Seven Grand

BEER SPECIALISTS

25 Laurel Tavern
23 York
   Father's Office
22 Library Alehouse
   Library Bar

BLUES/JAZZ CLUBS

27 Polo Lounge
25 Vibrato
23 Harvelle's
22 Catalina Jazz
19 Baked Potato

CELEB-SIGHTINGS

27 Polo Lounge
26 Mastro's Steak
   Chateau Marmont
   Bar Marmont
25 Shutters Lobby

CLUBS (DANCE)

23 Elevate
   Opera
   Boulevard 3
22 Social Hollywood
   King King

CLUBS (LIVE MUSIC)

23 Club Nokia
   Harvelle's
   El Rey Theatre
22 House of Blues
   Troubadour

COCKTAIL EXPERTS

27 Hotel Bel-Air
   Association
26 Peninsula Bar
25 Tiki-Ti
24 Seven Grand

DIVES

22 Burgundy Room
   HMS Bounty*
   Frolic Room
21 Bar 107
   Coach & Horses

DJs

25 Standard (Downtown)
23 Elevate
   Abbey
   Les Deux
22 King King

FINE FOOD TOO

27 Polo Lounge
26 Mastro's Steak
   Sidebar
   Bar Marmont
25 Vibrato

FIRST DATE

27 Hotel Bel-Air
   Association
26 Mastro's Steak
   Chateau Marmont
   Bar Marmont

GAY/LESBIAN

23 Abbey
21 East/West
19 here
   Akbar
18 Ultra Suede

* Indicates a tie with place above

HOTEL BARS

27 Hotel Bel-Air
   Polo Lounge
26 Chateau Marmont
   Peninsula Bar
25 Shutters Lobby

INDUSTRY SCENE

27 Hotel Bel-Air
   Polo Lounge
26 Mastro's Steak
   Chateau Marmont
   Peninsula Bar

JUKEBOXES

23 Griffin
22 Chalet
   HMS Bounty
21 4100 Bar
   Coach & Horses

NEWCOMERS (RATED)

27 Association
25 Laurel Tavern

23 Club Nokia
   Upper Manhattan
   Cuba Libre

SPORTS BARS

22 Tom Bergin's
20 Casey's
   Parlor
19 Hollywood Billiards
18 Barney's Beanery

TRENDY

27 Association
26 Edison Lounge
   Chateau Marmont
   Bar Marmont
25 Skybar

WINE BARS

23 Lou∇
22 Otheroom
   Bodega Wine
20 BottleRock
19 Air Conditioned

BY LOCATION

BEL-AIR/ BEVERLY HILLS

27 Hotel Bel-Air
   Polo Lounge
26 Mastro's Steak
   Sidebar
   Peninsula

CULVER CITY/WEST LA

23 Father's Office
20 BottleRock
19 Liquid Kitty
   Arsenal
18 Saints & Sinners

DOWNTOWN

27 Association
26 Edison Lounge
25 Standard (Downtown)
24 Seven Grand
23 Club Nokia

HOLLYWOOD

25 Hotel Café
24 Teddy's
23 Musso & Frank
   Tropicana
   Les Deux

LOS FELIZ

- 25 Tiki-Ti
- 23 Cuba Libre
- Dresden Room
- 21 Good Luck Bar
- 19 Drawing Room

SANTA MONICA/VENICE

- 25 Shutters
- 23 Chloe
- Father's Office
- Harvelle's
- McCabe's Guitar

SILVER LAKE

- 23 LAMILL
- 22 Spaceland
- Red Lion
- 21 4100 Bar
- Intelligentsia

WEST HOLLYWOOD

- 26 Chateau Marmont
- Bar Marmont
- 25 Skybar
- 24 Asia de Cuba
- Coco de Ville

Top Decor

- 28 Edison Lounge
- 27 Hotel Bel-Air
- 26 Vibrato
- Nine Thirty
- Shutters Lobby
- Peninsula Bar
- Association
- 25 Sidebar
- Polo Lounge
- Chateau Marmont

- Langham Huntington
- Tower Bar*
- Upper Manhattan*
- Skybar
- Asia de Cuba
- Social Hollywood
- Mastro's Steak
- 24 Boulevard 3
- Tiki-Ti
- Standard (Downtown)

Top Service

- 27 Hotel Bel-Air
- 26 Polo Lounge
- Mastro's Steak
- 25 Peninsula Bar
- Langham Huntington
- Vibrato
- 24 Sidebar
- York
- 23 Tiki-Ti
- Seven Grand

- Musso & Frank
- Shutters Lobby
- 22 Cuba LIbre
- King King
- HMS Bounty
- Drawing Room
- Three Clubs
- Tom Bergin's
- Dakota
- 21 Association

☑ Abbey

APPEAL | DECOR | SERVICE | COST
23 | 23 | 19 | E

West Hollywood | 692 N. Robertson Blvd. (Santa Monica Blvd.) |
310-289-8410 | www.abbeyfoodandbar.com

"You'll have a gay old time" at this "flamboyant" "Boystown mecca"
where all genders and orientations of "eye candy" are "welcome" to
"see, be seen" and "get drunk" off "expensive but generous pours" in
"labyrinthine" "indoor/outdoor" spaces to "lounge and dance" (for
privacy, grab a cabana and "close the curtains"); sometimes "tasty",
sometimes "mediocre" food's also served, but you might as well "forget dining" when it's "packed" and the "hot" staff becomes "distant."

NEW ADCB

▽ 22 | 22 | 19 | VE

West Hollywood | Mondrian Hotel | 8440 W. Sunset Blvd. (N. Olive Dr.) |
323-650-8999 | www.mondrianhotel.com

The recent rehab of WeHo's Mondrian hotel begot this lobby-set re-
joinder to its iconic poolside SkyBar; the lengthy, slinky space – all
creams, silvers and tangerine couches – provides a sufficiently swanky
setting for signature cocktails that hit high-end extremes, plus luxe
sushi from adjacent resto Asia de Cuba (after which the lounge is
named); despite the whiff of exclusivity, it's surprisingly of-the-
people: unlike its older sibling, there are no clipboard-toting bouncers.

Air Conditioned

19 | 16 | 17 | M

Santa Monica | 2819 Pico Blvd. (28th St.) | 310-829-3700
Venice | 625 Lincoln Blvd. (bet. Sunset Ct. & Vernon Ave.) | 310-230-5343
www.airconditionedlounge.com

"Slick, modern" digs and "casual, cool vibes" draw "eclectic" crowds to
this "spacious", "clubby" Venice "lounge to socialize", "booty shake"
or "listen to live music" and its "cozier" SaMo wine-bar sibling; though
there are many "friendly" servers to be found within, some complain
that "the guys out front suffer from 'doorman syndrome.'"

Airliner, The

▽ 18 | 18 | 15 | E

Lincoln Heights | 2419 N. Broadway (Ave. 24) | 323-221-0771

Its somewhat "rough" location notwithstanding, this rehabbed 1912
bi-level dance club/lounge with purple-and-black decor is an "upscale"
ticket for "dressed up" Lincoln Heights gentrifiers; however, those who
find the drinks "too expensive" and the bands playing in the second-
floor Mile High Club "too loud" "skip it and catch the next flight."

	APPEAL	DECOR	SERVICE	COST

Akbar
| 19 | 15 | 18 | M |

Silver Lake | 4356 W. Sunset Blvd. (Fountain Ave.) | 323-665-6810 |
www.akbarsilverlake.com

At once "the gayest straight bar and the straightest gay bar" in Silver
Lake, this "stress-free" spot baits a "mixed" "hipster clientele" with
"well-priced drinks" made by "friendly bartenders"; the main room is
home to a "killer jukebox", the rear features a dance floor, "missing
shirts" and the "smell of sweat", while "nonexistent decor" abounds.

Alibi Room
| 18 | 18 | 17 | M |

Culver City | 12236 W. Washington Blvd. (Campbell Dr.) | 310-390-9300 |
www.alibiroomla.com

"Tucked away in slow Culver City", this "trendy-looking" lounge with a
patio offers "hipper locals" a "relaxed" venue to down "reasonably
priced", "stiff drinks" and "strong beer choices" ferried by "friendly"
staffers; the addition of a kitchen manned by the folks behind the "fantastic" Kogi Korean BBQ taco truck has resulted in "a happy marriage."

NEW Apple Lounge
| - | - | - | VE |

West Hollywood | 665 N. Robertson Blvd. (Santa Monica Blvd.) |
310-358-9191 | www.applerestaurantlounge.com

Longtime roving LA promoter Allison Melnick hangs her velvet-roped
shingle in the long-ago Moomba space in the heart of Boystown; even
though it's a low-ceilinged, modestly sized, windowless basement, it's
a sizzling ticket for *The Hills* gals as well as Lindsay, Paris and the like.

Area
| 19 | 21 | 15 | VE |

West Hollywood | 643 N. La Cienega Blvd. (Melrose Ave.) | 310-652-2012 |
www.sbeent.com

Though it "has lost some of its luster" with the celeb set, this "small",
"swanky" midcentury-mod WeHo club is "still popular" with "beautiful
people" who don't mind being "judged by a bouncer"; indeed, the "attitude level" is as "high" as the drinks (made by "good looking bartenders
who are pretty much just good looking") and bottles are "pricey."

Arsenal, The
| 19 | 15 | 17 | M |

West LA | 12012 W. Pico Blvd. (bet. Bundy Dr. & Westgate Ave.) |
310-575-5511 | www.arsenalbar.com

"Maces, chain mail" and "artillery" lend "medieval charm" to this "divey", "pleasingly dark" West LA stronghold comprised of a front space

with a "tiny dance floor", a dining area where "decent bar food" is brought to table and a puffing "patio with heat lamps"; "stiff", "reasonably priced drinks" make it a "great spot to hit up on the fly."

☑ Asia de Cuba

24 | 25 | 21 | VE

West Hollywood | Mondrian Hotel | 8440 W. Sunset Blvd. (N. Olive Dr.) | 323-848-6000 | www.chinagrillmgt.com

It's "hard" to find a perch at this "hopping", "sultry", "everything-white" restaurant bar in the lobby of WeHo's "gorgeous" Mondrian Hotel, so "prepare to stand in those four-inch Louboutins" for quite some time; for your troubles you'll be rewarded with "fancy", "unique" cocktails, "fabulous" Asian-Cuban bites, "über-chic" compatriots and "unbelievable" views" from the patio – but you'll also be charged "celebrity prices."

☑ NEW Association, The

27 | 26 | 21 | E

Downtown | 110 E. Sixth St. (Main St.) | 213-627-7385

"One of the newest hidden treasures Downtown", this signless "speakeasy" denotes its presence with a "huge" front door that's an exact replica (right down to the brass lion knocker) of the one hanging at 10 Downing Street, the British Prime Minister's residence; inside, there's a "dark", "chill", "Sherlock Holmes"–meets-the-"'70s" vibe ("great carpet!"), with "expert mixologists" whipping up expensive, "stellar", "old-fashioned cocktails."

Avalon Hollywood

20 | 20 | 16 | E

Hollywood | 1735 N. Vine St. (bet. Hollywood Blvd. & Yucca St.) | 323-462-8900 | www.avalonhollywood.com

"Awesome" "global talent" spinning everything from pop to electronica depending on the night (which sometimes lasts "until the break of dawn") keeps this "historic" theater-turned–dance club a "Hollywood mainstay"; "good sightlines" and an "amazing sound system" also make it "great" for "hot" live shows, despite the "pricey drinks", service that could use some "improvement", "long lines and loads of people" ("sexy" as they may be).

Babe's & Ricky's Inn ⌀

- | - | - | I

Leimert Park | 4339 Leimert Blvd. (bet. 43rd St. & Vernon Ave.) | 323-295-9112 | www.bluesbar.com

"A little gem for live blues", this "funky", "down-home neighborhood joint" in Leimert Park has been owned and run by Laura Mae Gross since 1964; "great" acts "keep it real" Thursday–Saturday, but many fans feel that "it's best to go on Monday" for jam night and the free soul-food buffet; P.S. "don't forget your cash."

Baked Potato, The

19 | 13 | 19 | E

Studio City | 3787 Cahuenga Blvd. (bet. Lankershim Blvd. & Regal Pl.) | 818-980-1615 | www.thebakedpotato.com

"Drop in anytime" to this "legendary joint" in Studio City, because the live jazz is always "outstanding" and "cutting-edge", plus there are often "big stars" to be heard; the digs are "nothing fancy", the "only food on the menu" is hot spuds with "various stuffings" and the "cover seems to have gone up", but all that's of little concern to fans who cheer "long may it thrive!"

Bar, The

- | - | - | M

Hollywood | 5851 W. Sunset Blvd. (bet. Bronson & Van Ness Aves.) | 323-468-9154 | www.thebarhollywood.com

"Located on a forlorn stretch of Sunset", this Hollywood haunt *sans* signage lures hipsters and some celebs seeking a "relaxed, no-frills spot" for none-too-pricey drinks or a "little booth" in which to "hole up" with a sweetie; aesthetes appreciate the "cute bartenders", while remix-mavens keep an ear out for cred-toting local DJs.

NEW Barbarella Bar

- | - | - | M

Silver Lake | 2609 N. Hyperion Ave. (Griffith Park Blvd.) | 323-644-8000 | www.barbarellabar.com

Silver Lake gets a taste of the Sunset Strip with this flashy new resto-lounge filled with candles, a hand-carved wood bar, leather upholstery and a dance floor; $300 Grey Goose bottle service is available, but there are also midpriced creative cocktails and two dozen draft beers to wash down the Eclectic eats; N.B. the sole nod to its namesake flick is the barmaids' sexy black corsets.

Barcopa

18 | 14 | 17 | M

Santa Monica | 2810 Main St. (bet. Ashland Ave. & Hill St.) | 310-452-2445

"Come early if you want a seat" ("there aren't too many"), otherwise "be prepared to stand" at this "dark", virtually "hidden" SaMo club – or just dance with the "diverse crowd" of "cool people" getting "sweaty" to "an excellent mix" of music on the "pretty darn small" floor while loosening up with "strong", "well-priced" drinks.

		APPEAL	DECOR	SERVICE	COST

NEW Bar Delux

∇ | 19 | 17 | 13 | E

Hollywood | 1624 N. Cahuenga Blvd. (Hollywood Blvd.) | 323-461-6800 | www.bardelux.com

The Cahuenga Corridor meets the Jazz Age at this Hollywood den whose design conceit could be described as 'zigzag moderne', with the centerpiece being an enormous emerald-green stained-glass mural featuring zeppelins and airplanes behind the bar; the cocktails are as top-tier as the promoters, meaning the velvet rope might not be so friendly unless you're on the list – or a gorgeous miss.

NEW Bardot

∇ | 21 | 21 | 17 | VE

Hollywood | Avalon | 1737 N. Vine St. (bet. Hollywood Blvd. & Yucca St.) | 323-462-1307 | www.bardothollywood.com

"Even guys" should "wiggle into something teeny and black" to breach the tougher-than-tough door at this "'it' spot of the moment" in the old Spider Club space; if you get in, you might catch a burlesque show, a "celebrity DJ" (Ryan Gosling has hit the decks here) or a surprise live performance; if nothing else, it's a "place to dance and be seen" – even if it is "a little too Hollywood."

Bar Lubitsch

21 | 21 | 20 | E

West Hollywood | 7702 Santa Monica Blvd. (bet. Spaulding & Stanley Aves.) | 323-654-1234

"The vodka menu is off the charts" at this watering hole in WeHo's Little Russia, which flaunts an "Eastern Euro vibe" with "beautiful", red-heavy decor; "sexy, intelligent" comrades "get there early to reserve a table" in the front bar area, order "amazing drinks" from the "low-attitude" servers, then hit the "rocking" rear dance floor where "awesome DJs" spin.

☒ Bar Marmont

26 | 24 | 20 | VE

West Hollywood | 8171 Sunset Blvd. (Crescent Heights Blvd.) | 323-650-0575 | www.chateaumarmont.com

"After all these years", this "iconic", "chichi" WeHo "retreat" still pulls in "hipsters", "out-of-towners" and "wannabes" looking to "rub elbows with celebs" in a "gorgeous, step-back-in-time space" with multiple rooms and an "amazing garden", but "without belittling lines or insane covers"; in that same vein, the staffers exhibit "no pretentions" as they ferry "solid cocktails" and "yummy" European-influenced nibbles ("very expensive" yet "worth every cent").

	APPEAL	DECOR	SERVICE	COST

☑ Barney's Beanery
18 | 15 | 17 | M

West Hollywood | 8447 Santa Monica Blvd. (bet. Holloway & Olive Drs.) | 323-654-2287 | www.barneysbeanery.com

"Thankfully, some things never change", such as this "delightfully cheese-tastic" WeHo "frat-boy heaven" where "rowdy" capacity crowds "scream" to be heard over "lots of TVs", "video games, air hockey, pool tables" and karaoke; there's a "huge list" of "reasonably priced" beers, plus "greasy" "cheap eats" off a menu as big as the "Sunday *Times*" – but be warned: you might "have to wait forever" to get them.

Bar NINETEEN12
23 | 24 | 20 | VE

Beverly Hills | Beverly Hills Hotel | 9641 Sunset Blvd. (Crescent Dr.) | 310-273-1912 | www.barnineteen12.com

"Stylish" and "welcoming", this "expensive" Beverly Hills Hotel lounge is "perfect for getting to know someone new, catching up with old friends" or enjoying a "quiet drink" alone since it's so "intimate" and "the music is not loud"; its "cozy" interior and covered terrace are just as "sophisticated" and "upscale" as the "beautiful people" who patronize them.

Bar Noir
▽ 24 | 23 | 21 | VE

Beverly Hills | Maison 140 Hotel | 140 S. Lasky Dr. (Durant Dr.) | 310-281-4000 | www.maison140.com

Beverly Hills hot shots say this "small, charming" bar in hotel Maison 140 delivers a feeling of "exclusivity"; festooned with "swanky" red, black and white furnishings (Chinoiserie, Lucite, French stuff), the lobby-adjacent space is quite "quiet and intimate", so if you choose it for a "first date", make sure you have plenty of talking points at the ready.

Bar 107
21 | 18 | 19 | M

Downtown | 107 W. Fourth St. (Main St.) | 213-625-7382

"Self-aware of its divey-ness, but still cool", this "tight" Downtown "blast" houses "kitschy" paraphernalia such as '80s video games and a photo booth; "super-cool bartenders" sling "not-pricey drinks", while on certain evenings, "pretty rad DJs" spin "ass-shaking" tracks in the rear.

Beauty Bar
17 | 17 | 15 | E

Hollywood | 1638 N. Cahuenga Blvd. (bet. Hollywood Blvd. & Selma Ave.) | 323-464-7676 | www.beautybar.com

Though "neither the martinis nor the manicures are that great", "girls love" the two-for-one "deals" at this Hollywood saloon/salon done up in "kitschy", "'60s" style; yes, it "smells like nail polish" and it often gets "ridiculously packed", but "great music mixes from the past" that incite "spontaneous dancing" are pluses.

Belmont, The
19	17	18	E

West Hollywood | 747 N. La Cienega Blvd. (Sherwood Dr.) | 310-659-8871 | www.thebelmontcafe.com

"Go early" for a spot in the "awesome outdoor area" of this WeHo resto-lounge that offers half-off apps and drinks 4–7 PM, "spot-on music" and "sassy" staffers; "after happy hour ends", it gets even more "crowded" with "young and noisy" types – indeed, it's "one step above a fraternity party", but at least it's a "classy" step (expensive too).

Bigfoot Lodge
23	23	19	M

Atwater Village | 3172 Los Feliz Blvd. (bet. Garden Ave. & Glenfeliz Blvd.) | 323-662-9227 | www.bigfootlodge.com

Possibly the "raddest place" in Atwater Village, this "low-key" hangout "amuses" with an animatronic "Smokey the Bear" sentry and "log-cabin theme", not to mention "cheapish beers" and "tasty" signature cocktails; "great music" is always on offer, as are "fun theme nights" like Sunday bingo ("the best way to forget" Monday is imminent).

Boardner's
21	17	20	M

Hollywood | 1652 N. Cherokee Ave. (bet. Hollywood Blvd. & Selma Ave.) | 323-462-9621 | www.boardners.com

"You might rub tushies with someone famous" as you make your way to the "huge", "hangout"-worthy booths at this "cool, relaxed", "historic" Hollywood "dive that isn't really a dive"; the bar employs "attentive" 'tenders to pour "strong", "mighty tasty", "fairly priced" drinks, the kitchen concocts "great" grub and the attached B52 Club hosts "fashion shows, bands", dancing and more.

Bodega Wine Bar
22	22	20	M

Santa Monica | 814 Broadway (Lincoln Blvd.) | 310-394-3504
Pasadena | Paseo Colorado | 260 E. Colorado Blvd. (bet. Garfield & Marengo Aves.) | 626-793-4300
www.bodegawinebar.com

"Shared tables encourage conversation with strangers" just as "affordable" prices promote "palate-testing" at these "sleek" Pasadena and SaMo wine bars that also offer "dark", "private corners with couches" and "simple" noshes; oenophiles "question" a place where "everything is the same price" ($8 a glass, $21 a carafe, $32 a bottle), and while some end up saying "yay!", others conclude it's "not for the connoisseur."

Bonaventure Brewing Co.

	19	16	19	E

Downtown | Westin Bonaventure Hotel | 404 S. Figueroa St., 4th fl. (4th St.) | 213-236-0802 | www.bonaventurebrewing.com

For "happy-hour beers or that long lunch you really don't want to end", Downtown office workers join hotel guests at this pub-grub-purveying microbrewery in the Westin Bonaventure; the interior is strictly "cookie-cutter", but the "awesome" patio "on the fourth-floor pool deck" boasts "nice views" of the surrounding Financial District towers.

Bordello

	22	22	19	M

Downtown | 901 E. First St. (Vignes St.) | 213-687-3766 | www.bordellobar.com

With "lushly colored" ornate decor that's an "homage" to its brothel past, this "cool little spot" is "a feast for the eyes" and, if you're not in Downtown's industrial district, "worth" the "trek"; "sexy bartenders" who serve "strong drinks for a good price" add to the "decadent fun", as does the "great lineup" of live acts and other events.

BottleRock

	20	17	21	E

Culver City | 3847 Main St. (bet. Culver & Venice Blvds.) | 310-836-9463 | www.bottlerock.net

There's a "magnificent idea" behind this Culver City wine bar/shop: as long as you "order at least two glasses", the "helpful servers" will open any one of the "hundreds of bottles" in stock, a worldly selection displaying "all different price points"; there's "decent" nibbles to boot, but the "uncomfortable stools" and "sterile" decor have some positing "it'd be a home run" if only it were given "a proper lounge setting."

Boulevard 3

	23	24	18	E

Hollywood | 6523 W. Sunset Blvd. (bet. Shrader Blvd. & Wilcox Ave.) | 323-466-2144 | www.boulevard3.com

"Vegas meets Hollywood" at this "high-energy" "palace" that "has it all": "glitz, glamour and good-looking people"; the "gorgeous" environs include "plenty of lounge areas, several bars", VIP balconies, an "amazing dance floor" and a "chill patio" on which cabanas flank a reflecting pool and a fireplace ("beautiful touch"); scene-seekers, though, admit "disappointment" that the "huge space dilutes" the potential for A-list potency.

Brass Monkey
20 | 16 | 19 | E

Koreatown | 3440 Wilshire Blvd. (Mariposa Ave.) | 213-381-7047

"LOL" at this "dark, old-school" Koreatown "karaoke super-spot" that's "always fun" whether "the tunes being belted out" are "concert-quality" or "painful"; if there's "a two-hour wait to sing", kick back with the "laid-back, come-as-you-are" crowd and work on that two-drink minimum (management is "pushy" about enforcing it, but there's no cover).

Brig, The
18 | 16 | 16 | M

Venice | 1515 Abbot Kinney Blvd. (Venice Blvd.) | 310-399-7537

Though "nothing special" designwise ("is this New Jersey?"), this "modern dive" has a lock on "young, fun" Venetians thanks to its "decent music", pool table and, perhaps most importantly, "large, free adjacent parking lot"; indeed, it's "a lively spot to hit up post-work" as well as late-night, but it "can be a hassle to get a drink when it's crowded."

Broadway Bar
21 | 20 | 19 | M

Downtown | 830 S. Broadway (bet. 8th & 9th Sts.) | 213-614-9909 | www.broadwaybar.la

"Before or after a show at the Orpheum", mingle with Downtown loft-dwellers at this "relaxed" yet "dynamic" "drinking destination" "in a historic building"; "lovely old LA decor" abounds on two floors featuring "a huge circular bar" where "you can see what's happening all around you" and a balcony overlooking the "less-than-desirable" street outside.

Bull Pen
∇ 17 | 14 | 20 | M

Redondo Beach | 314 Ave. I (bet. Elena Ave. & PCH) | 310-375-7797

You "gotta love" the bands booked at this Redondo Beach "throwback" and the way they get the "50-plus crowd" to pack its "tiny dance floor"; even those who find evenings here "marginal" admit they're bullish on its "reasonably priced drinks", while "beef eaters" say the food's "good."

Bungalow Club, The
20 | 20 | 18 | E

Melrose | 7174 Melrose Ave. (bet. Detroit St. & Formosa Ave.) | 323-964-9494 | www.thebungalowclub.com

"Alluring assets" abound at this Melrose resto-club with an "attractive" ground-level bar and dining room, a "great second floor for larger private parties" plus dancing to "cool music" and a "large", "candlelit", "heated patio" with "private cabanas" "draped in sheer white fabric"; "awesome" mojitos and martinis complement the "international food menu", all of which bean-counters deem "decently priced."

Burgundy Room   22 | 17 | 19 | M

Hollywood | 1621½ N. Cahuenga Blvd. (bet. Hollywood Blvd. & Selma Ave.) | 323-465-7530

"Get real drunk" for a "decent price" at this "divey", "dark-as-hell", "last bastion of old Cahuenga" in ever-gentrifying Hollywood; when the "punkers" and "rock 'n' rollers" who keep it "perpetually crowded" get too "rowdy", "the bartenders do a great job of handling" them, while the "crew of rotating DJs" distracts them with "excellent spins."

Cabana Club   20 | 22 | 17 | E

Hollywood | 1439 Ivar Ave. (bet. De Longpre Ave. & Sunset Blvd.) | 323-463-0005 | www.cabanaclubhollywood.com

"Macho doormen" man the lines at this Hollywood magnet for "girls in skimpy clothes" and other "young" clubgoers mixing and "mingling" on two separate dance floors, one set on an "expansive" palm tree–lined terrace encircled by a "beautiful" reflecting pool; no surprise, "drinks are on the pricey side" (bottle service and private cabanas don't come cheap either), and though it's "still considered a hot spot", the less-impressed find the scene "only a shadow of what it used to be."

Café-Club Fais Do-Do ⌖   ▽ 22 | 14 | 20 | M

Mid-City | 5257 W. Adams Blvd. (bet. S. Cloverdale Ave. & S. Redondo Blvd.) | 323-931-4636 | www.faisdodo.com

Music lovers sing the praises of this "ramshackle dive bar" in Mid-City, where "mind-blowing" blues, rock and soul bands come together with Cajun-Creole eats and "cheap, cold beer"; though its off-the-beaten-path locale is a deterrent to some, fans insist a pilgrimage pays off with a convivial atmosphere that sums up "good, clean fun."

Cameo Bar   ▽ 25 | 25 | 23 | VE

Santa Monica | Viceroy Santa Monica | 1819 Ocean Ave. (Pico Blvd.) | 310-451-8711 | www.viceroysantamonica.com

"Fancy without being stuffy", this "lush" retreat in the Viceroy Santa Monica boasts a "stunning" Hollywood Regency design rich with earthy browns and grassy greens; come "well dressed", "join the party at the bar" where "friendly bartenders" whip up "great cocktails" or "enjoy the show" from one of the couches – just make sure you're "financially prepared"; P.S. the "beautiful poolside lounge" exudes similar "class."

Canyon Club

| 19 | 15 | 17 | E |

Agoura Hills | Whizins Ctr. | 28912 Roadside Dr. (Cornell Rd.) | 818-879-5016 | www.canyonclub.net

If they're "still around", yesteryear's "best music and comedy performers" gig at this "intimate", "no-frills", supper-club-like concert venue in Agoura Hills; even cynics who feel it's the place "those bands you used to love go to die" admit it can still be "a lot of fun", though it's "kinda pricey", and "to ensure a table", you have to commit to dinner (consensus is the "food is secondary").

Casey's Irish Bar & Grille

| 20 | 19 | 19 | M |

Downtown | 613 S. Grand Ave., downstairs (bet. 6th St. & Wilshire Blvd.) | 213-629-2353 | www.bigcaseys.com

Downtown office workers head to this atmospheric pub for "well-priced" pints and "decent" Irish grub served amid dartboards, a pool table and "plenty of TVs" blaring Eurocentric sports; it's also "convenient" for a drink "before a concert" at the nearby Music Center, but regulars note that while it fills up during "happy hour", on weekends it "can be a ghost town."

Catalina Jazz Club

| 22 | 20 | 21 | E |

Hollywood | 6725 W. Sunset Blvd. (bet. Cherokee & Highland Aves.) | 323-466-2210 | www.catalinajazzclub.com

"Jazz is king" at this "lively, grown-up" Hollywood supper club showcasing "top-notch" talent including "lots of famous artists" plus a "good showing of newer acts"; yes, "drinks are pricey" and "covers are steep", but the starry-eyed swear "when the lights go down and the band kicks in, you're transported to another time"; N.B. a full dinner menu is also on offer.

Cat & Fiddle

| 22 | 20 | 19 | M |

Hollywood | 6530 W. Sunset Blvd. (bet. Highland & Wilcox Aves.) | 323-468-3800 | www.thecatandfiddle.com

"U.K. expats" "playing darts", "random celebrities" keeping it "low-key" and "every Hollywood assistant" having a "birthday" or "going-away party" are just some of the "diverse" peeps who keep this "super-chill" English "standby" "ridiculously crowded"; the "spacious" interior's as "authentic" as the "well-priced" pints and "solid pub fare", but the "amazing", "lovely" "patio is where it's at."

Central   - | - | - | VE

Hollywood | 1710 N. Las Palmas Ave. (Hollywood Blvd.) | 323-871-8022 | www.sunsethollywood.com

Nightcrawlers find nothing to detract from their own fabulousness at this minimally outfitted, brown-on-brown Hollywood lounge whose centerpiece is a spray of bare branches sprouting along a dramatically tall wall; though not as A-listy as it once was, it still courts bottle-buyers with constantly shifting promoted nights.

Cha Cha Lounge   19 | 19 | 17 | M

Silver Lake | 2375 Glendale Blvd. (Brier Ave.) | 323-660-7595 | www.chachalounge.com

"Eastside grit" is on proud display at this "boisterous" Silver Lake "true dive" whose "island theme" seems "half-assed" when viewed alongside the "funny Mexican kitsch" and "more flannel than your eyes can handle" (it may be "the most hipster place of all!"); when not "playing foosball" or "taking pics in the photo booth", folks chug "PBR on tap" and "average priced" cocktails dispensed from a "grass hut" bar.

Chalet, The   22 | 21 | 20 | M

Eagle Rock | 1630 Colorado Blvd. (Townsend Ave.) | 323-258-8800

"A mix of hipsters, yuppies" and Occidental College kids packs this Eagle Rock bar whose "ski lodge–themed" looks "transport you to a winter hideaway" in the "Swiss Alps"; a "cozy fireplace" and an "amazing jukebox" boost the appeal, as do the "cheap" yet "generous pours"; P.S. try it on a weeknight, because on weekends it's usually "bursting at the seams."

⌘ Chateau Marmont Lounge   26 | 25 | 21 | VE

West Hollywood | Chateau Marmont | 8221 W. Sunset Blvd. (bet. Crescent Heights Blvd. & Sweetzer Ave.) | 323-656-1010 | www.chateaumarmont.com

"J'adore le Chateau!" goes the refrain coming from this "small lobby bar and its adjacent garden terrace", "sophisticated" "oases of gentility and old-world charm" in WeHo; it's "happening" "any night of the week" (and "catnip for first dates"), but it's such an "exclusive" "star zone", "you'd better be famous or a hotel guest to get in" – and be toting big bucks to boot; N.B. its sibling, the Bar Marmont, is at the base of the hill.

Chloe
`23` `23` `19` `E`

Santa Monica | 1449 Second St. (bet. B'way & Santa Monica Blvd.) | 310-899-6999 | www.barchloe.com

"There's no sign" outside this "hidden" SaMo "gem" flaunting "pretty" luxe French deco touches and populated by a "cool", well-heeled crowd; "speakeasy-style" cocktails match the "elegant", "intimate" vibe that's "perfect for a date" or a night of "witty conversation" with friends, while the bar bites mean imbibers won't go hungry.

Clear
▽ `15` `19` `13` `E`

Studio City | 11916 Ventura Blvd. (Carpenter Ave.) | 818-980-4811 | www.clearlounge.net

Valley "locals" looking to kick back and "cozy up to strangers" say this Studio City lounge comes through with a "cool" crowd and "beautiful" mod design featuring white vinyl walls and chocolate-brown banquettes; detractors decry the "cheesy" vibe, though "cute" bartenders redeem, and even if it's not quite Hollywood, many insist it "has the potential" to come close.

NEW Club Nokia
`23` `22` `19` `E`

Downtown | LA Live | 800 W. Olympic Blvd. (Figueroa St.) | www.clubnokia.com

"Great headliners" attract a "diverse crowd" to this "hip", "modern" new concert venue in Downtown's LA Live complex, where the setup is so "intimate", "no matter where you sit or stand you can see the show"; "incredible sound and lights" add to its appeal, as does the "huge bar", even though its wares are "pricey."

Coach & Horses ⊅
`21` `14` `20` `M`

Hollywood | 7617 Sunset Blvd. (bet. Fairfax Ave. & Gardner St.) | 323-876-6900

"Old-school cool" is alive and well at this "classic" Hollywood dive, a "down-to-earth" "neighborhood bar with character" catering to an eclectic mix of Stripgoers; the jukebox is solid, and drinks are served up "quick" and relatively cheap – just "bring cash" since credit cards aren't accepted ("if you forget", there's an ATM on-site).

	APPEAL	DECOR	SERVICE	COST

Cock 'n Bull ⊅

19 | 15 | 21 | M

Santa Monica | 2947 Lincoln Blvd. (Ashland Ave.) | 310-399-9696
"It probably helps to be British" to appreciate this "real" Santa Monica
pub where an expat crowd sips "cheap" pints and throws darts while
"watching Manchester United take on Chelsea on the telly"; live salsa
and karaoke on weekends are less-authentic touches, though the congenial mood means it's "always a good bet" no matter what's going on.

Coco de Ville

24 | 22 | 17 | E

West Hollywood | 755 N. La Cienega Blvd. (Waring Ave.) | 310-659-3900 |
www.theonerestaurants.com
An A-list crowd digs the "see-and-be-seen" vibe at this compact club
attached to STK in WeHo; though its offerings are pretty "typical" (DJ,
bottle service), the "whimsical", colorful design stands out, and regulars report it's a "fun" place, if you can get past the velvet rope.

Cohiba

∇ 18 | 16 | 19 | E

Long Beach | 110 W. Broadway (Pine Ave.) | 562-491-5220 |
www.cohibalongbeach.com
"Smoke a stogie", shoot some pool or hit the dance floor at this Long
Beach club whose "basic loungey design is conducive to both "cou-
ples" and singles on the prowl; regulars warn the cover can be a "little
expensive" for the area, while the overall mood "depends on what
night you go", whether for hip-hop DJs or live R&B.

Comedy Store

20 | 12 | 15 | E

West Hollywood | 8433 W. Sunset Blvd. (N. La Cienega Blvd.) |
323-650-6268 | www.comedystore.com
At this "intimate" Sunset Strip chuckle hut, Pauly Shore and his mom
book both famous and "up-and-coming comics"; "service is catch-as-
catch-can", the digs are "dark" and "tired", the "drinks are weak" and
"you'll have to drop some cash" to make the cover and the minimum,
but it mostly "serves its purpose" – you'll "laugh your butt off."

NEW Conga Room, The

21 | 20 | 16 | VE

Downtown | LA Live | 800 W. Olympic Blvd. (S. Figueroa St.) |
213-749-0445 | www.congaroom.com
"Salsa into the wee hours" at this "enticing", "boisterous" Latin dance
club, which celebrity backers have relocated from the Miracle Mile to
Downtown's LA Live; notable architects and artists contributed to the

"amazing" environs, which include Pan-Latin eatery Boca and "crowded bars" from which it can be "tough to get" the "overpriced" drinks.

NEW Copa d'Oro
▽ 21 | 19 | 22 | VE

Santa Monica | 217 Broadway (bet. 2nd & 3rd Sts.) | 310-576-3030 | www.copadoro.com

Cocktail culture and the locavore movement come together at this "innovative" SaMo newcomer where mixologists craft "delicious", expensive drinks from "fresh" fruits and herbs straight from the "farmer's market"; the Med-style digs get busy on "weekends", though a doorman out front keeps the crowds in check and maintains the "nice vibe" inside.

NEW Corkbar
- | - | - | E

Downtown | 403 W. 12th St. (Grand Ave.) | 213-746-0050 | www.corkbar.com

Downtown's South Park district (adjacent to the Staples Center and LA Live) welcomes this high-ceilinged, modern vino venue, located in one of the new eco-friendly loft developments sprouting up in the 'hood; the focus is on pricey California wines – with more than 40 by the glass and dozens more by the bottle – accompanied by vittles like charcuterie sandwiches, shrimp risotto and cheese.

Crimson
▽ 23 | 21 | 16 | E

Hollywood | 1650 Schrader Blvd. (Hollywood Blvd.) | 323-960-3300 | www.crimsonhollywood.com

The more hard-rocking half of a Hollywood nightlife duo (Opera's on the other side of the wall), this "fun", bottle-service-pushing lounge with a small dance floor bathes a "trendy crowd" in red hues as it cradles them in plush couches amid furry walls; but since it's "exclusive in who it allows in", those left out in the cold dis it's "snobby and overrated."

NEW Crocker Club, The
- | - | - | E

Downtown | 453 S. Spring St. (5th St.) | 213-239-9099 | www.thecrockerclub.com

A bank vault in Downtown's Historic Core has been fashioned into this "intriguing" subterranean lounge harboring "still-intact security boxes", massive restored doors and private rooms; service is "friendly", but to experience it, you'll have to adhere to the dress code (i.e. "slick hair and a dark striped 'going out' shirt" for guys) – a prerequisite that seems "stuffy" to some.

	APPEAL	DECOR	SERVICE	COST

NEW Crown Bar
22 | 22 | 18 | E

West Hollywood | 7321 Santa Monica Blvd. (N. Fuller Ave.) | 323-882-6774 | www.crownbarla.com

"Have big bucks" or be "a hottie" to get into this "swanky", "exclusive" lounge in WeHo's Little Russia, where "delicious apps, tasty tonics" and plenty of "pomp" are offered amid a "beautiful" wood-paneled oval bar, red-leather booths, mirrors and miniature sconces; indeed, it's "popular and the staff knows it", so be on your guard for "unnecessary attitude."

NEW Cuba Libre
23 | 22 | 22 | E

Los Feliz | 1745 N. Vermont Ave. (Kingswell Ave.) | 323-661-5900

"Beautiful, hip people" indulge in mojitos and sustenance straight out of Havana at this "brilliant" Los Feliz cafe/bar offering "great" half-off happy-hour specials; "there's really nothing Cuban" about the decor (gilt-frame mirrors above dark-brown leather booths, hanging potted plants), but authenticity reemerges in the "sexy" DJ-spun salsa.

Daily Pint
18 | 10 | 18 | M

Santa Monica | 2310 Pico Blvd. (bet. Cloverfield Blvd. & 23rd St.) | 310-450-7631

If "you don't have a lot of moola, but need a cold one", pop into this "glorious dump" in SaMo for a choice of "dozens of beers, including some not-so-standards" and "lots of scotches"; stay for "foosball, shuffleboard and billiards", and come "unshaven" – it's "unpretentious."

NEW Dakota
22 | 23 | 22 | E

Santa Monica | 1026 Wilshire Blvd. (11th St.) | 310-393-8200 | www.dakotalounge.com

"Part lounge, part club", this "expensive" new SaMo venue decked in fiery red hues "separates" its "multiple personalities", which "makes conversation much easier" for those who haven't come for the DJs or live acts; Eclectic bites can be enjoyed at the couches, but it may be best to "stake out a spot at the bar" for prompt cocktails from the harried but "warm 'tenders."

Del's Saloon
▽ 16 | 11 | 17 | M

West LA | 12238 Santa Monica Blvd. (bet. Bundy Dr. & Wellesley Ave.) | 310-207-1978 | www.delssaloon.com

"When you want to be loud and rowdy", grab your "pool-playing" "lush friends" and "come as you are" to this "run-down" West LA dive serving "strong", "cheap drinks"; there's karaoke on Wednesday and Saturday nights, and "you'll be surprised by how good the singers are."

Dime, The
| 19 | 13 | 17 | I |

Fairfax | 442 N. Fairfax Ave. (bet. Beverly Blvd. & Melrose Ave.) | 323-651-4421

"Squeeze into" this "dime-sized" Fairfax "hole-in-the-wall-but-not-really" to "hang without spending a lot of money" alongside "trendy" folks grooving to "awesome music"; but if you're irked by "jam-packed" digs and sometimes "rude" service, you'll "wonder why you bothered."

Drawing Room ∌
| 19 | 11 | 22 | I |

Los Feliz | 1800 Hillhurst Ave. (Melbourne Ave.) | 323-665-0135

"Slum it in Los Feliz" at this "small", "dank", "laid-back" dive employing a "cool staff" to pour "cheap drinks" for an "always-interesting crowd"; "karaoke Sundays are a great way to end the week", while any day can be started here, since it "opens at 6 AM" – "now that's hard-core!"

Dresden Room
| 23 | 19 | 20 | E |

Los Feliz | 1760 N. Vermont Ave. (bet. Kingswell & Melbourne Aves.) | 323-665-4294 | www.thedresden.com

"A must-visit", this "kooky" "place to forget what year it is" in Los Feliz still provides "cheesy fun" via the "nostalgic sounds of "amazing", "adorable" "singing duo Marty and Elayne, fixtures for years and years" and true "living legends"; "basic drinks" and food are also on offer, as are regularly scheduled open-mike nights.

Eagle Los Angeles ∌
| ▽ 25 | 18 | 26 | I |

Silver Lake | 4219 Santa Monica Blvd. (Hoover St.) | 323-669-9472 | www.eaglela.com

"Leather boys, bears and their admirers" comprise the "friendly" ("maybe a little too") crowd at this Silver Lake gay "institution" sporting "decent tunes" and decor that's, well, "you don't go for the decor"; it may be a bit "ersatz" in its roughness, but the drinks are "cheap."

East/West Lounge
| 21 | 23 | 20 | E |

West Hollywood | 8851 Santa Monica Blvd. (N. San Vicente Blvd.) | 310-360-6186 | www.eastwestlounge.com

"If you're gay and looking for upper-class love in WeHo", sidle into this "grown-up lounge" with "plush" furnishings, "clever mirror placement and chic color coordination"; it's got "members, but everybody is treated like a welcome guest" by the "eager-to-please" staff, which doles out "indulgent", "expensive drinks."

NEW Ecco

19	19	17	E

Hollywood | 1640 N. Cahuenga Blvd. (Hollywood Blvd.) | 323-464-2065 | www.eccohollywood.com

"Everybody's trying to be green" nowadays, and this "interesting", "tight" Tinseltown club takes it to the max with tons of eco-friendly innovations; everyone says the energy-saving sound system is "great" and the low-wattage LED lighting (most evident in a glowing grid above the dance floor) is "awesome" – too bad the service and the vibe are still "typical Hollywood."

Echo, The

22	14	20	M

Echo Park | 1822 W. Sunset Blvd. (bet. Glendale Blvd. & Lemoyne St.) | 213-413-8200

Echoplex, The

Echo Park | 1154 Glendale Blvd. (bet. Park Ave. & Sunset Blvd.) | 213-413-8200
www.attheecho.com

"Diamonds in the rough" of Echo Park, these conjoined live-music twins "consistently book" "quality acts" ranging from "rock and dance" to "reggae", "old-school punk" and beyond; the space is "scruffy" and the "bathrooms are tiny", but covers are usually "cheap" and the drinks are "reasonably priced", plus there's "a smoking area with picnic tables out back."

☑ Edison Lounge, The

26	28	21	E

Downtown | 108 W. Second St. (bet. Main & Spring Sts.) | 213-613-0000 | www.edisondowntown.com

"Sparks of genius" abound in this "inspired reimagining" of a "huge" subterranean power plant, a Downtown "fantasy" lounge that's earned LA's No. 1 Decor rating thanks to its "awesome" "1920s industrial" setting with "nooks and crannies to explore", "strange black-and-white movies" "projected on the walls" and "sensual" lighting; the "fantastic", "pricey drinks" are sometimes "slow" coming, but the "sharp-looking" crowd ("adhere to the dress code!" beg stylistas) finds "enticing" distraction in an "eclectic" mix of music or the "quirky entertainment."

	APPEAL	DECOR	SERVICE	COST

El Carmen
20 | 20 | 19 | E

Crescent Heights | 8138 W. Third St. (bet. Crescent Heights Blvd. & S. La Jolla Ave.) | 323-852-1552

"Know what you're getting" when you step into this "epitome of kitschy fun" in Crescent Heights, and "you'll like what you get": "stiff", "yummy margs" made with an "amazing tequila" selection and "delicious" snacks served amid "Mexican wrestler decor"; "perpetually crowded" digs are the norm ("get there early, it's small"), but since there's "no attitude", "relaxation" is virtually guaranteed.

El Cid
20 | 18 | 18 | E

Silver Lake | 4212 W. Sunset Blvd. (bet. Bates & Myra Aves.) | 323-668-0318 | www.elcidla.com

"Descend the stairs" of this Silver Lake "time machine" and enter a world of "charming", "classic Spanish flavor" where "great" flamenco shows are staged and "to-die-for" sangria, margaritas, tapas and full dinners are served; when the dancers are resting their stompers, "a completely mixed-bag" of bands, DJs, comedians and open-mikers fills the entertainment bill.

Elevate Lounge
23 | 24 | 18 | E

Downtown | 811 Wilshire Blvd., 21st fl. (S. Flower St.) | 213-236-9600 | www.elevatelounge.com

"Girls in itty-bitty dresses and false lashes" have a greater chance breaching the "selective" velvet rope of this "sleek" indoor/outdoor aerie with "gorgeous views of Downtown"; if you make it up, get down to "awesome" DJ spins on the dance floor or plop on one of the surrounding "comfy couches" to "elevate your spirits" via "yummy", "pricey drinks."

Eleven
21 | 22 | 18 | E

West Hollywood | 8811 Santa Monica Blvd. (bet. Larrabbee St. & Palm Ave.) | 310-855-0800 | www.eleven.la

Prepare to be "visually assaulted" by "some of WeHo's hottest", most "well-coiffed" boys as well as "handsome" bartenders "*sans* shirts" and "acrobatic" go-go boys ("excuse me sir, why did you kick my drink over?") at this "swellegant", "modern" restaurant-cum–gay dance club; the "great" cocktails are "expensive", but nightcrawlers say they cost "no more than anywhere else" nearby.

El Rey Theatre

	APPEAL	DECOR	SERVICE	COST
	23	20	17	E

Mid-Wilshire | 5515 Wilshire Blvd. (bet. Burnside & Dunsmuir Aves.) |
323-936-6400 | www.theelrey.com

This "awesome old theater" along Mid-Wilshire's Miracle Mile makes
available its "stunning" art deco digs (with "great sound" and "swell
sightlines" throughout) to often-"fantastic" "up-and-coming bands";
though discerning booze-hounds dis "so-so drinks", most realize that
the main appeal lies in the venue's "intimate", "classy vibe."

Ercole's ⌷

	APPEAL	DECOR	SERVICE	COST
	20	12	20	I

Manhattan Beach | 1101 Manhattan Ave. (11th St.) | 310-372-1997

"Wear anything more than jeans, a T-shirt and flip-flops, and you're
overdressed" for this "quintessential" Manhattan Beach dive where
"surfer dudes and their surfer gals" "sit at decades-old tables" or the
"stripped-down bar" and chug "inexpensive" quaffs ("don't expect
martinis", and don't try paying with a credit card); the "pool table in
the back gets lots of action", as does the "enjoyable jukebox."

Falcon

	APPEAL	DECOR	SERVICE	COST
	21	24	19	E

Hollywood | 7213 W. Sunset Blvd. (Alta Vista Blvd.) | 323-850-5350 |
www.falconslair.com

"Hip and so Hollywood", this somewhat "hidden" resto-lounge snags
"pretty people" with an "amazing indoor/outdoor" space that man-
ages to be "sexy", "classy" and "homey" all at once; the "food's actu-
ally good" for such a "scene", but it's the "pricey, potent drinks" – not
to mention the "excellent music" – that really "rock the house."

⊠ Father's Office

	APPEAL	DECOR	SERVICE	COST
	23	18	17	E

Culver City | 3229 Helms Ave. (Venice Blvd.) | 310-736-2224
Santa Monica | 1018 Montana Ave. (bet. 10th & 11th Sts.) |
310-393-2337
www.fathersoffice.com

The "cramped" SaMo patriarch of LA's Most Popular nightlife duo is a
real "pain in the butt": you must wait on "long" "lines to get in", "wran-
gle a busy bartender to order", "pounce on" a "first-come, first-
served" seat and eat while "hovering vultures" "wait for your table";
but it's "definitely worth" the "hassle" for its "cornucopia of specialty
beers" and "out-of-this-world hamburgers"; P.S. the Culver City off-
spring is "more spacious", and therefore often "less stressful."

	APPEAL	DECOR	SERVICE	COST

Faultline ⦵
▽ 26 | 17 | 27 | I

Silver Lake | 4216 Melrose Ave. (Vermont Ave.) | 323-660-0889 |
www.faultlinebar.com

"Sport serious five o'clock shadow, don your tightest leather and pump those pecs" ("piercings and tats are pluses") at this Silver Lake spot where "punks, daddies, bears and other homo riffraff" congregate for theme parties like beer busts and buzz nights ("prepare to be sheared"); hot 'n' heavy "hanky-panky" happens inside, while breathers are taken on a "patio with the ambiance of a prison yard."

NEW Fifth, The
- | - | - | M

Valley Village | 4821 Whitsett Ave. (Riverside Dr.) | 818-753-8297

Nightlife vet Craig Trager (NoBAR, The Well, The Woods) invades Valley Village with this dark, spiffed-up strip-mall bar where twenty-something single suburbanites belly up for midpriced brewskis before considering the jukebox selections, which range from Pearl Jam and Guns N' Roses to Operation Ivy and Alice in Chains; the flat-screens flash ESPN, and the sole pool table is put to near-constant use.

Firefly
24 | 24 | 21 | E

Studio City | 11720 Ventura Blvd. (Colfax Ave.) | 818-762-1833

For a "Hollywood vibe" with "Valley convenience", head to this "dark, sexy" Studio City lounge "tucked away" behind an ivy-covered facade; the "library-style" interior creates a "mellow" mood suited for "catching up with a close friend over a fabulous glass of wine", while the open-air smoking area overlooking a fire pit is conducive to "pickups"; P.S. there's also a menu to "complement the wide array" of pricey cocktails.

Footsie's
- | - | - | M

Highland Park | 2640 N. Figueroa St. (Ave. 26) | 323-221-6900

Expect "cheap drinks, good tunes, pool tables" and a patio at this "out-of-the-way hideaway"; set in slowly gentrifying Highland Park, the "onetime local dive now caters to a different, hipper crowd", which marvels that "it's almost more comfortable the more people there are" here.

Formosa Café
20 | 19 | 20 | E

West Hollywood | 7156 Santa Monica Blvd. (La Brea Ave.) | 323-850-9050

"Slip into a booth and you slip back in time" at this circa-1939 WeHo "legend" offering "echoes of a long-forgotten Hollywood" in its "dark", "moody" atmosphere; though some sigh it's showing its age and "losing its appeal", it still draws a steady stream of "hipsters", "tourists" and other assorted "hangers-on" in search of strong drinks and a "nostalgic" LA vibe; N.B. in warm weather, try the rooftop patio.

4100 Bar
21 | 21 | 19 | M

Silver Lake | 4100 W. Sunset Blvd. (Manzanita St.) | 323-666-4460
"Get hit on by a hot hipster" at this "awesome, little" Silver Lake "oasis" with "lush, red genie-bottle" decor, lots of "intimate nooks" and "low lighting" that ensures "everyone looks good"; a "fantastic jukebox" provides the beat as "friendly", "attentive" 'tenders sling midpriced drinks, but if you "want a seat" to sip them, "get there early", as it's often "packed shoulder-to-shoulder."

Foxtail
23 | 23 | 18 | E

West Hollywood | 9077 Santa Monica Blvd. (Doheny Dr.) | 310-859-8369 | www.sbe.com/foxtail
"Be someone or know someone" to cut through the "tough" ropes at this "dark, sexy", art deco/nouveau-speckled WeHo dance lounge with so many "flashbulb-worthy" "celeb sightings", "it feels like an episode of *TMZ*"; "creative", "mouthwatering" specialty drinks are "made for you by mixologists" using "top-shelf" booze – and you better believe they're "expensive."

Frank 'n Hank ⌀
- | - | - | I

Koreatown | 518 S. Western Ave. (bet. 5th & 6th Sts.) | 213-383-2087
Snow, the longtime owner/manager, keeps the beer cold and "cheap" at this cash-only Koreatown dive; Eastside hipsters and stars in stealth-mode join neighborhood boozehounds for video poker, electronic darts, televised sports and yesteryear melodies that emanate from a jukebox.

Frolic Room
22 | 15 | 19 | M

Hollywood | 6245 Hollywood Blvd. (bet. Argyle Ave. & Vine St.) | 323-462-5890
"One part Hollywood hipsters, one part theatergoers and one part regular" "barflies" is the clientele recipe for this "classic", "no-frills", "dirty-delicious" dive "right next door to the Pantages"; sure, "it's seen better days", but "deep roots" in many a surveyor's "personal history" ensure it's going and will continue to go "strong."

	APPEAL	DECOR	SERVICE	COST

Fubar

18 | 15 | 18 | E

West Hollywood | 7994 Santa Monica Blvd. (bet. Crescent Heights Blvd. & Fairfax Ave.) | 323-654-0396 | www.fubarla.com

"Ogling boys in jockstraps" and "explicit videos" while "squeezing onto a pathetic platform of a dance floor" is how you roll at this "crazy", "sleazy-in-a-great-way" Boystown gay "dive with expensive drinks" and "scandalous" theme nights; some sensitive surveyors want to "see a therapist for post-traumatic stress disorder" the morning after, but it may be a futile endeavor – "some things you just can't unsee."

Gallery Bar

– | – | – | E

Downtown | Millennium Biltmore Hotel | 506 S. Grand Ave. (5th St.) | 213-624-1011 | www.millenniumhotels.com

Downtown's "classic" Millennium Biltmore Hotel is the setting for this "old-school bar" featuring Renaissance-esque chandeliers that hang from "beautiful carved-wood ceilings" and "sofas for lounging and cuddling"; the "excellent martinis" include one named after legendary murder victim the Black Dahlia (it's purported to be her final tippling place), while high-end sushi comes courtesy of Pan-Asian eatery Sai Sai.

Garter, The

∇ 17 | 14 | 20 | M

Venice | 2536 Lincoln Blvd. (Washington Blvd.) | 310-577-3741 | www.thegartervenice.com

"No cover", daily happy hours, a "sexy atmosphere and good drinks" get "LMU and UCLA coeds" to "pour into" this "fun, low-key place" to "grind on the dance floor", "hang and listen to music" in Venice; there are times when it's "kind of empty", but when it's "packed", it's totally "hot."

Golden Gopher, The

22 | 20 | 20 | M

Downtown | 417 W. Eighth St. (bet. Hill & Olive Sts.) | 213-614-8001 | www.goldengopher.la

"In a shady area of Downtown", "hipsters" and "after-workers" burrow into this "dark" "faux dive" for "stiff, well-priced drinks" amid "cool '80s arcade games" and "small statues" of – you guessed it – golden gophers; "relaxation"-seekers get "stoked" when they "catch it on a mellow night", but more often than not, it's "crowded and loud"; P.S. it possesses a "coveted takeaway license", so you can grab a "six pack on the way out."

	APPEAL	DECOR	SERVICE	COST

Gold Room, The

`-` `-` `-` M

Echo Park | 1559 W. Sunset Blvd. (bet. Echo Park Ave. & Galveston St.) | 213-482-5259

As if "good tunes, cheap beer" and $1 tequila shots weren't enough to draw Echo Park hipsters into this onetime solely Mexican dive, there are also fab "freebies" like tacos and bottomless bowls of peanuts; when attendant DJs aren't spinning Prince off of their Macs, a roving band of mariachis stops in to play a set by the front door for old times' sake.

Good Luck Bar

21 22 19 M

Los Feliz | 1514 Hillhurst Ave. (Hollywood Blvd.) | 323-666-3524

With "dim lighting" that makes everyone look "sexy", you're bound to have good luck at this "cozy", "comfy Los Feliz hangout" festooned with "quirky, fun" red chinoiserie and "cool sofas"; "friendly, efficient bartenders" pour "the whole gamut of cocktails" to ignite libidos, but it's also a "great place to grab a beer with your buddies", as there's usually no problem "hearing one another talk."

Grand Star Jazz Club

∇ 20 15 19 VE

Chinatown | 943 Sun Mun Way (Jung Jing Rd.) | 213-626-2285 | www.grandstarjazzclub.com

"Teeming with cool cats and weirdoes" looking for "a good time", this bare-bones Chinatown music venue presenting everything from jazz to rap to R&B is "as un-Hollywood as you can get"; it's pretty "chill" when there's a show, but when it hosts "hipster dancing" and the popular Firecracker hip-hop party every other Friday, the vibe is "off-the-hook."

Green Door

20 23 17 E

Hollywood | 1429 Ivar Ave. (Sunset Blvd.) | 323-463-0008

Fading French "glamour" is the "beautiful" decor theme of this "chic" lounge where "the usual Hollywood" "pretty people" "pack the dance floor" and "great patio"; it's often "guest-list-only, so make friends with a promoter", and while you're waiting for your "pricey" drink, remember it's a "place to be seen, not served."

Griffin, The

23 24 21 M

Atwater Village | 3000 Los Feliz Blvd. (Boyce Ave.) | 323-644-0444 | www.thegriffinlounge.com

"Harry Potter" fans "feel like a Hogwarts collegian every time" they come to this "dungeonlike lair" in Atwater Village, with "lots of seating" in

red leather booths, fireplaces and arched brick ceilings; a "great juke-box" entrances the "cool" crowd, while the "big patio" entices smokers to take their "great drinks" (concocted by "über-hot" staffers) outside.

Guy's

∇ 24 | 17 | 19 | E

Crescent Heights | 8713 Beverly Blvd. (bet. Robertson & San Vicente Blvds.) | 310-360-0290 | www.guysbar.com

Following time off for a thorough redo, this Crescent Heights A-list vet is back and still "worth it for celebrity-elbow-rubbing" while imbibing "expensive drinks"; however, you'd better have oodles of "self-worth" to join the entrance queue (especially if you're not on the guest list), otherwise some members of the door staff "may ruin your desire to go in."

Gypsy Café

18 | 19 | 16 | E

Westwood | 940 Broxton Ave. (bet. Le Conte & Weyburn Aves.) | 310-824-2119 | www.gypsycafe.com

"Poet-types" who dig hookah pipes help turn this Mediterranean restaurant with "some outdoor seating" into a "popular nightspot" with "great people-watching"; it's also a "trendy" "UCLA hangout", getting so "loud" with coeds "having a blast", you might not be able to "hear your own thoughts."

NEW Halo

- | - | - | VE

Hollywood | 1743 N. Cahuenga Blvd. (Hollywood Blvd.) | 323-463-1237 | www.halohollywood.com

The aura of classic Hollywood glamour radiates from this new velvet-rope-bound, bottle-service-pushing club in the space formerly inhabited by Ritual; nothing less than an answered prayer will get you past the gatekeepers and into the black, white and glass-bubble chandelier-bedecked space, which is slated to be augmented by an easier-to-breach sports bar post-Survey.

Hal's Bar & Grill

22 | 20 | 21 | E

Venice | 1349 Abbot Kinney Blvd. (California Ave.) | 310-396-3105 | www.halsbarandgrill.com

A Venice "classic", this "lively", "noisy" "hang" is known for its signature martinis, wide-ranging New American menu and "sophisticated" painting-adorned interior; despite its status as an "art-scene" mainstay, staffers are "warm" and the vibe "unpretentious", so most agree it's "always a pleasure"; N.B. there's also live jazz Sundays and Mondays.

	APPEAL	DECOR	SERVICE	COST

Happy Ending, The
- - - M

Hollywood | 7038 W. Sunset Blvd. (N. Sycamore Ave.) | 323-469-7038 |
www.thehappyendingbar.com

The heartland comes to Hollywood via this ambitious sports bar catering to coeds, post-grads and never-grads with 30 flat-screens and a mélange of other multimedia, including video games and a photo booth; bachelorette and birthday parties are big, as is the menu of midpriced standbys (think chicken skewers, fish tacos and po' boys), but its most popular attribute is an impressively frat-tastic innovation: a drink wheel spun hourly to determine the next special.

Harvelle's
23 14 19 M

Santa Monica | 1432 Fourth St. (bet. B'way & Santa Monica Blvd.) |
310-395-1676 | www.harvelles.com

Catch blues, bongos and jazz at this Santa Monica "mecca" for live music that's "been around forever" (since 1931, in fact); perhaps some find its "dark", "dingy" digs less than appealing, but drinks are "cheap" and covers are relatively "low", so for most it's a solid bet for an entire "night's worth of entertainment"; P.S. don't miss Sunday's "sexy" burlesque show.

here
19 21 19 E

West Hollywood | 696 N. Robertson Blvd. (Santa Monica Blvd.) |
310-360-8455 | www.herelounge.com

"Upscale WeHo clones" "mix with other interesting" gay men at this "trendy" "half-indoor, half-outdoor" lounge with a "small dance floor", "great lighting" and "contemporary", "minimalist" design; depending on the night, the atmosphere can be "sexually charged" or "more social", while on some evenings, like Truck Stop Fridays, it's packed with "the highest density of lipstick lesbians" around.

Hideout, The
17 12 19 E

Santa Monica | 112 W. Channel Rd. (PCH) | 310-429-1851 |
www.santamonicahideout.com

"Mellow locals wet their whistle" at this "chill" Santa Monica lounge just a block from the beach; though "low-stress" most nights, it gets "crowded and sceney on weekends" when DJs spin Top 40 tunes "late into the night" and a "drunk, post-college" crowd takes over the dance floor; N.B. free tacos are served at Thursday's karaoke party.

| | APPEAL | DECOR | SERVICE | COST |

HMS Bounty
22 | 18 | 22 | M

Koreatown | 3357 Wilshire Blvd. (bet. Alexandria & Kenmore Aves.) |
213-385-7275 | www.thehmsbounty.com

"Kitsch galore" fills this K-town dive/eatery that's a "step back in time",
from the "nautical" decor to the "great staff" that seems like it was
"around for the Gold Rush" to the "diverse" clientele (including the
requisite "hipsters"); "strong" drinks are poured for "deal" prices (ditto
the food) and provide the perfect excuse to drop cash into the "awesome
jukebox" and "belt out some Lionel Richie with your drunk friends."

Hollywood Billiards
19 | 15 | 19 | M

Hollywood | 5750 Hollywood Blvd. (Taft Ave.) | 323-465-0115 |
www.hollywoodbilliards.com

"One of the few billiards halls in Hollywood", this "warehouse"-like
sports bar features 30 tables and a video arcade plus plenty of HDTVs
perfect for "watching the game with fellow fans"; cold beer and "cheap
eats" complete the offerings.

Hollywood Canteen
18 | 18 | 19 | E

Hollywood | 1006 N. Seward St. (bet. Romaine St. & Santa Monica Blvd.) |
323-465-0961 | www.hollywoodcanteenla.com

At this "cozy" drinking-and-eating spot, a remake whose vintage-
picture-strewn decor "tries hard to connect" to the 1942 original
launched by Bette Davis and John Garfield, an Air-Stream trailer sits off
a "large patio" – but "make no mistake", you'll find "no trailer trash here";
indeed, the crowd is "cool", even when sweating on the small dance floor.

Hop Louie
∇ 18 | 16 | 19 | I

Chinatown | 950 Mei Ling Way (bet. Jung Jing Rd. & Lei Min Way) |
213-628-4244

Though it "feels like a basement" circa "1971", Eastsiders "always have
fun" after Chinatown gallery openings at this "no-frills" bar set in an
ornamental pagoda; the rocking jukebox is another draw, as is the
"cheap" selection of "stiff drinks" like camptastic scorpion bowls.

⧉ Hotel Bel-Air Bar
27 | 27 | 27 | VE

Bel-Air | Hotel Bel-Air | 701 Stone Canyon Rd. (Sunset Blvd.) | 310-472-1211 |
www.hotelbelair.com

If you want to "impress" or "hobnob" with "civilized" "jetsetters", you
can't do better than this "serene" Hotel Bel-Air "treasure" – voted

No. 1 for both Appeal and Service; it delivers "romance" via a "lovely", "lap-of-luxury" lounge filled with "lots of wood, leather", a "wonderful fireplace" and "spectacular" staffers, especially the evening pianist and "bartenders who take the craft seriously" (their wares are "pricey" but "worth it").

Hotel Café

25 | 20 | 19 | M

Hollywood | 1623½ N. Cahuenga Blvd. (bet. Hollywood & Sunset Blvds.) | 323-461-2040 | www.hotelcafe.com

"You could be listening to the next big thing" when you check into this "comfortable", "intimate live-music venue", a "laid-back", "friendly" "change of pace from the typical Hollywood social scene" presenting "fantastic" acts at "a fraction of the price" of many competitors; P.S. the entrance is through a "tiny door" in a rear alley.

ⓩ House of Blues

22 | 21 | 17 | E

West Hollywood | 8430 W. Sunset Blvd. (Olive Dr.) | 323-848-5100 | www.hob.com

Still one of the "hottest" tickets in town for live shows, this Sunset Strip link of the national meals-and-music chain is cherished for its "intimate" setup that "makes you feel as if you're a friend of the band"; "weak" drinks and "hordes of tourists" may detract from the experience, but diehards declare it's all "worth it just to see the talent."

NEW h.wood

- | - | - | VE

Hollywood | 1738 N. Orange Dr. (bet. Franklin Ave. & Hollywood Blvd.) | 323-871-2262 | www.thehwood.com

Nightlife impresario Amanda Demme, who made her name with Teddy's and the Tropicana Bar down the street, oversees this sprawling, luxury-priced indoor/outdoor Tinseltown club with an unusual location in a formerly disused corner of Hollywood & Highland; the industrial-chic decor is highlighted by bricks and windows reclaimed from Andy Warhol's NY Factory, which makes the whole shebang look like an '80s warehouse dance party.

Hyde Lounge

23 | 21 | 16 | VE

West Hollywood | 8029 W. Sunset Blvd. (bet. Crescent Heights & Laurel Blvds.) | 323-656-4933 | www.sbeent.com

Though "not as popular as it used to be", if you go to this still "exclusive", "intimate" Hollywood lounge "on the right night, with the right promoter", you might still spy "celebrities" canoodling in its "elegant", "dark corners"; some trend-watchers opine its "15 minutes" are nearly "over", but that doesn't mean it's any cheaper – you still need lots of "cash to throw around."

Improv
22 | 16 | 18 | M

Melrose | 8162 Melrose Ave. (bet. N. Kilkea Dr. & N. La Jolla Ave.) | 323-651-2583 | www.improv.com

Settle into your "cheap vinyl seat" and prepare to talent scout at Melrose's "granddaddy" of comedy clubs, because the wits "you see today may be starring in their own TV shows tomorrow"; "unexpected drop-ins" are not unheard of, and while some surveyors have been saddled with "washed-up" talent and "watered-down drinks" (you must purchase at least two), most assure "lots of giggles" are the norm.

Insomnia Cafe ∌
20 | 17 | 19 | E

Fairfax | 7286 Beverly Blvd. (bet. N. Alta Vista Blvd. & N. Poinsettia Pl.) | 323-931-4943

"Shhh, don't interrupt the roomful of writers clicking away" "lest you be bludgeoned by a MacBook" at this "old-school" Fairfax-adjacent coffee shop whose self-enforced, librarylike silence also makes it "great" for "reading or studying"; "comfy couches" are available until 1:30 AM nightly – "the only bummer" is that the WiFi isn't free anymore.

Intelligentsia
21 | 18 | 19 | I

Silver Lake | 3922 W. Sunset Blvd. (Hyperion Ave.) | 323-663-6173 | www.intelligentsiacoffee.com

Silver Lake is the appropriate setting for this "hipster coffee shop" where "incredible" espresso, cappuccino and lattes are "expertly crafted" by "experienced baristas"; "creative" types and nondrinkers make their own "funky" nightlife scene on the "nice patio" Thursday–Saturday when it closes at 11 PM, but more folks appreciate it as a "morning-after cure."

Jimmy's Lounge
∇ 22 | 20 | 23 | E

Hollywood | 6202 Santa Monica Blvd. (El Centro Ave.) | 323-957-1066

Habitués of this Hollywood haunt say it "doesn't draw a huge crowd" (at least during the week), but that doesn't make it any less "awesome" – on the contrary, they can usually get a "group of friends" together here hassle-free; the "small" space sports brown-on-brown and stripper-pole accents, while outside there's a "large patio" on which to "chill."

| | APPEAL | DECOR | SERVICE | COST |

Joint, The
▽ 16 | 14 | 16 | M

Pico-Robertson | 8771 W. Pico Blvd. (bet. Robertson Blvd. & Wooster St.) | 310-275-2619

The sound's cranked "way too loud" at this Pico-Robertson venue, which makes its live rock sets "not to be missed" for "sensory overload"–seekers; drinks can help you forget about the somewhat "sterile" environs when they're "over-poured", but have the converse effect when they're "under-poured."

Jumbo's Clown Room
21 | 13 | 18 | M

Hollywood | 5153 Hollywood Blvd. (Winona Blvd.) | 323-666-1187 | www.jumbos.com

For "skanky" "hilarity", clown around in this bikini bar that could have been "created by David Lynch", a "grungy, small and oddly shaped" dive where "go-go" gals with "tattoos you won't forget" perform "strange", "must-see" routines around a "single pole"; it's "fun for men and women alike", but needless to say, "not a place to take mother."

Key Club
19 | 15 | 16 | E

West Hollywood | 9039 W. Sunset Blvd. (bet. Doheny Dr. & Hammond St.) | 310-274-5800 | www.keyclub.com

"Everything you need for a wild night out" is provided at this WeHo venue: mostly "fabulous music acts", "great sightlines", "lots of space to move around", "top-notch sound and lighting" and "well-made drinks"; a "comfortable second-floor lounge" serving food is another plus – so what if the decor's only "ok" and service can be "slow"?

King Edward Saloon ⌀
- | - | - | I

Downtown | 131 E. Fifth St. (Los Angeles St.) | 213-629-2023

Downtown's loft-dwelling gentrifiers occasionally stop into this, the oldest bar on Skid Row, for an urban-adventure with "down-and-out" types; it's a "fun place to go" at 6 AM (that's when it opens) if you need a cheap drink, a roast-beef sandwich and some TV time.

King King
22 | 15 | 22 | M

Hollywood | 6555 Hollywood Blvd. (bet. N. Hudson & Whitley Aves.) | 323-960-9234 | www.kingkinghollywood.com

"Still an unpretentious gem" in Hollywood, this "house-music" bastion gives "serious dancers" "lots of space" while allowing them to "get up-close and personal with the spinning maestros"; though the "high-ceilinged", "industrial" space sports "not much in the way of decor", it does offer "strong drinks" from "attentive bartenders who move as quickly as they can considering how crazy-busy it gets"; P.S. "eclectic" live bands and cabaret are regularly scheduled.

NEW Kitchen 24

- | - | - | M

Hollywood | 1608 N. Cahuenga Blvd. (Selma Ave.) | 323-465-2424 | www.kitchen24.info

Midpriced American eats are doled out 24/7 at this Hollywood eatery whose scene becomes dishier the later it gets; the look is a mod update of a retro diner with white terrazzo floors, brown leather seating, pink piping and a huge U-shaped bar mixing up mimosas and margaritas as well as more imaginative libations like the Jalapeñargarita.

Knitting Factory Hollywood

19 | 14 | 17 | M

Hollywood | Galaxy Theater Mall | 7021 Hollywood Blvd. (Sycamore Ave.) | 323-463-0204 | www.knittingfactory.com

"There's always a surprise" at this "big" Tinseltown music venue, where the "young, old, normal, weird, hipster, punk and prep" converge to check out "lots of bands playing in different rooms" while getting lit via a "typical selection" of libations ("the bartenders try to keep up"); it's "kind-of-run-down" and has a "weird location in a mall", yet it remains "always crowded."

NEW Lab, The

- | - | - | M

Downtown | 3500 S. Figueroa St. (Jefferson Blvd.) | 213-743-1843

The lush life hits the laboratory at this USC-backed Downtowner that also welcomes nonstudents; its science theme is slickly conjured with formula-filled chalkboards, communal tables and beakers that hold some of the 40 moderately priced brews on offer (including a couple of exclusives from San Diego's Karl Strauss Brewing Company), while experiments with gastropub fare are administered for moderate prices.

La Cita

19 | 15 | 21 | M

Downtown | 336 S. Hill St. (bet. 3rd & 4th Sts.) | 213-687-7111 | www.lacitabar.com

Downtowners have commandeered this "dark, divey" Mexican ranchero bar and turned it into something of a "hipster haven" because they're *loco* about the "eclectic" tunes, "multiple" spots to dance, large tequila selection, "good beers" and "ok prices"; when inside gets *caliente,* they hit the "jumping patio" to "get some fresh air" "down-wind of the smokers."

LAMILL
23 | 21 | 19 | M

Silver Lake | 1636 Silver Lake Blvd. (Effie St.) | 323-663-4441 | www.lamillcoffee.com

Coffee is elevated to an "art form" at this "luxe" Silver Lake beanery presenting "unique" brews alongside an "expensive" menu crafted by the chef and pastry chef of Hollywood's Providence restaurant; though some are smitten by its flashy red-and-gold-flecked contempo-rococco decor, others find the overall package "too pretentious" for the neighborhood; N.B. it's BYO for now, but a beer and wine license is in the works.

☒ Langham Huntington Bar
25 | 25 | 25 | VE

Pasadena | Langham Huntington Hotel & Spa | 1401 S. Oak Knoll Ave. (bet. Hillcrest Ave. & Ridge Way) | 626-568-3900 | pasadena.langhamhotels.com

Enjoy a "slower pace" at this "elegant", "refined" lounge in a "classy" Pasadena hotel; "sit outside on the patio and have a cigar" while taking in views of the Horseshoe Gardens or join your fellow "well-heeled" "sophisticates" inside where live piano or jazz often fills the air – either way, it feels like something "out of an old movie."

Largo
∇ 19 | 17 | 18 | M

West Hollywood | 366 N. La Cienega Blvd. (bet. Beverly Blvd. & Oakwood Ave.) | 310-855-0350 | www.largo-la.com

Alt-pop and -comedy followers' "second living room" has moved from Fairfax to the old Coronet Theater in WeHo, with "amazing" Friday night singer-songwriter staple Jon Brion in tow; the main venue may not be as "reasonably priced" and "intimate" as it once was (there's a smaller space dubbed the Little Room), but there's still "great sound", plus an "excellent" "no-cell-phone, no-talking policy" during the show; P.S. a liquor license is coming "any day now."

Laugh Factory
21 | 16 | 18 | E

Hollywood | 8001 Sunset Blvd. (N. Laurel Ave.) | 323-656-1336 | www.laughfactory.com

"Sit in front and you will be targeted" at this Hollywood ha-ha house, but it's worth the risk, especially if a "famous comic shows up to do an impromptu set" ("big headliners" command "pricey" covers – and "good luck getting in without reserved tickets"); "claustrophobic" surveyors heckle the "tight quarters", which are patrolled by "pushy waitresses" who "make sure you take your two-drink minimum."

NEW Laurel Tavern

25 | 22 | 20 | M

Studio City | 11938 Ventura Blvd. (bet. Carpenter & Radford Aves.) | 818-506-0777 | www.laureltavern.net

Belly up to the bar and order a "juicy burger" or one of the many craft beers on tap at this "fantastic new Studio City gastropub that's "quickly become a favorite among locals"; moderate tabs and congenial staffers give it a "friendly" ambiance, though regulars warn it's best enjoyed off-hours before the "young fraternity crowd" crams in.

LAX

21 | 20 | 16 | VE

Hollywood | 1714 N. Las Palmas Ave. (Hollywood Blvd.) | 323-464-0171 | www.laxhollywood.com

Though possibly "passed its peak" as a "see-and-be-seen" A-lister, this Hollywood hangar is now "hyped" mainly as "a big meat market for early twentysomethings" who "crowd" the "small dance floor", "celeb-seek" and sip "horrendously overpriced" drinks brought by staffers who "could at least try to be a little nicer" than if they worked at a real airport.

Les Deux

23 | 23 | 18 | VE

Hollywood | 1638 N. Las Palmas Ave. (bet. Hollywood Blvd. & Selma Ave.) | 323-462-7674 | www.dolcegroup.com

"Big, big fans" "love, love" the "hot, hot" scene at this "awesome" Hollywood "playground for the rich and famous" with "terrific DJs" and "comfortable" furnishings that make it feel "like an upscale house party", both inside and on the "great patio"; foes, on the other hand, say it has "jumped the shark", as evidenced by all the "C-list celebrities" and "wannabe scenesters trying to get on *TMZ*" or "*The Hills.*"

Library Alehouse

22 | 18 | 20 | M

Santa Monica | 2911 Main St. (bet. Ashland Ave. & Marine St.) | 310-314-4855 | www.libraryalehouse.com

Hopsheads hail this "homey" Santa Monica pub boasting an "overwhelming" array of suds, including "one of the best selections of Belgian and German beers this side of the English Channel"; its "comfort-

| | APPEAL | DECOR | SERVICE | COST |

food" menu also earns kudos, as does its "mellow and beachy" terrace offering a "pleasant" respite from the "crowds" inside.

Library Bar
22 | 22 | 20 | M

Downtown | Library Court Lofts | 630 W. Sixth St. (S. Hope St.) | 213-614-0053 | www.librarybarla.com

"Popular" after work, this "cozy" Downtown bar pulls in a "shoulder-to-shoulder" crowd of "suits and locals" for "creative cocktails", "premium" Belgian beers and "tasty" snacks like pork belly skewers and peppered fries; true to its name, it's furnished in a "bookish" style, with handsome leather couches and a tome-filled wall; N.B. happy hour runs weekdays from 3–8 PM.

Library Coffeehouse
∇ 22 | 24 | 21 | M

Long Beach | 3418 E. Broadway (bet. Newport & Redondo Aves.) | 562-433-2393

A heavily gay clientele "feels at home" at this "relaxing" Long Beach java joint boasting free WiFi and an "awesome", "living room–like" setting filled with "shelves lined with tomes" (many "out-of-print" and on sale for just $1); open until midnight (1 AM on weekends), it's "a great place to end the night with a cafe mocha and a biscotti" away from the "typical club scene."

Liquid Kitty
19 | 15 | 21 | M

West LA | 11780 W. Pico Blvd. (bet. Barrington Ave. & Bundy Dr.) | 310-473-3707 | www.liquidkitty.com

"If you don't care to see whom you're talking to", "what you're drinking" or where, feel your way into this "super-dark" West LA "hole-in-the-wall"; "cool", "friendly" staffers shake up and serve "a multitude of delicious", "hella-strong" martinis to the beat of "great music", which comes via either karaoke, "DJs or live bands."

Little Bar
- | - | - | M

Mid-Wilshire | 757 S. La Brea Ave. (bet. 8th St. & Wilshire Blvd.) | 323-937-9210 | www.littlebarlounge.com

"New Englanders feel right at home" watching the Sox at this "awesome little Boston bar" in Mid-Wilshire; some almost-fans recommend "it would improve greatly by investing in a flat-screen or two", but let's face it, "after a couple of rounds" of "moderately priced beer" or "creative soju mocktails", "any fuzziness in the TV is strictly self-inflicted."

| | APPEAL | DECOR | SERVICE | COST |

Little Joy Cocktail Lounge ∅
V 21 | 11 | 23 | I

Echo Park | 1477 Sunset Blvd. (Portia St.) | 213-250-3417

Yes, this Echo Park spot is a "sparse" "dump", but it's an "incredible" one – or so say the "hipsters" who make it a "mecca" for "ever-flowing PBR" and other "cheap" libations; the "young" clientele is "less rambunctious" than you might expect for there being pool tables and "loud music" perpetually emanating from the "great jukebox."

Little Temple
V 18 | 17 | 19 | M

Silver Lake | 4519 Santa Monica Blvd. (Virgil Ave.) | 323-660-4540 | www.littletemple.com

Though acolytes suspect this "sweet spot" is "largely unknown" outside of Silver Lake, you wouldn't know it from the way the "dance floor gets packed" with "young, mixed, laid-back" peeps; the Asian-inspired setting features candles flickering against Buddha heads, bamboo-lined walls and plenty of places to lounge with moderately priced cocktails.

Lou
V 23 | 21 | 24 | M

Hollywood | Melrose Place | 724 N. Vine St. (bet. Camerford & Melrose Aves.) | 323-962-6369 | www.louonvine.com

Small-production wines pair with farmstead cheeses and unusual small plates at this "quirky" Hollywood wine bar where an "attentive" staff guides you through the ever-evolving selection of vinos; despite its "nondescript" locale in an anonymous strip mall, it draws a steady stream of "hip" oenophiles who appreciate the "intimate" vibe.

L Scorpion
V 21 | 21 | 20 | E

Hollywood | 6679 Hollywood Blvd. (Las Palmas Ave.) | 323-464-3026 | www.scorpionhollywood.com

"A must-visit for its legendary tastings" culled from an "amazing tequila selection", this Mexican restaurant with a "tight", "dark", Gothic-looking setting (wrought-iron fixtures, arches, exposed brick) is "a great stop on a Hollywood Boulevard crawl" anytime; the wares are "a little pricey", but the "friendly, knowledgeable staff" mitigates the sting.

Lucky Baldwins
20 | 14 | 19 | M

Pasadena | 17 S. Raymond Ave. (bet. E. Colorado Blvd. & E. Green St.) | 626-795-0652 | www.luckybaldwins.com

"If you're aching for merry ol' England", try your luck at this "divey" pub in Pasadena proffering a "wide selection of beers on tap" including "hard-to-find Belgians", "decent food" and soccer matches broadcast at odd hours; sensitive noses complain the interior "smells like too many nights of drinking gone wrong" and recommend "sitting on the patio", while insiders counter "beware of the smoke" wafting in from outside.

Mama Juana's Latin Lounge
APPEAL	DECOR	SERVICE	COST
-	-	-	E

Studio City | 3707 Cahuenga Blvd. (Regal Pl.) | 818-505-8636 | www.mamajuanas.com

Dinner and dancing get a Latin spin at this "fun" Studio City supper club boasting a "great", "large dance floor" where patrons samba, salsa, merengue and more to the strains of live bands; amateurs and experienced steppers alike come early for lessons that not only provide admission for the rest of the evening, but may even be taught by a pro who appeared on *Dancing With the Stars*.

Mandrake
APPEAL	DECOR	SERVICE	COST
∇ 21	18	21	M

Culver City | 2692 S. La Cienega Blvd. (bet. Venice & Washington Blvds.) | 310-837-3297 | www.mandrakebar.com

"If you weren't looking for it, you'd never know" where to find this "arty", "decently priced" "hole-in-the-wall" catering to Culver City's thriving gallery scene; the environs – "all cement" and wood – are "unpretentious", just like the "knowledgeable bartenders", who really know how to make a "stiff" one; P.S. also on offer are "tasty snacks", a "roomy, pleasant patio", exhibits, readings and screenings.

ⓩ Mastro's Steakhouse
APPEAL	DECOR	SERVICE	COST
26	25	26	VE

Beverly Hills | 246 N. Cañon Dr. (bet. Dayton Way & Wilshire Blvd.) | 310-888-8782 | www.mastrosrestaurants.com

This "old-school" "place to impress" in Beverly Hills greets guests with an entry-level bar where they can "unwind before enjoying" an "incredible" steak dinner, and a "happening" second-floor lounge for listening to piano music afterward (or instead of); just as "dramatic" as the scene ("starlets" hunting for "sugar daddies" and vice versa) are "huge", "stiff" martinis "cooled by dry ice", not to mention the "high prices."

Match
APPEAL	DECOR	SERVICE	COST
-	-	-	M

North Hollywood | 4657 Lankershim Blvd. (Kling St.) | 818-766-0116 | www.matchnoho.com

"A gem" along a North Hollywood stretch of auto dealerships, this signless lounge offers a "chill" place for nearby studio and production-house after-workers to gather "without feeling pretentious" ("gotta love" the PBR on tap!); Jeffrey Best, who also owns nearby Firefly, employs a staff of "real people" and has done a "beautiful" job decorating the place with banana plants, ceiling fans and votives.

Mayan, The
19 | 19 | 15 | E

Downtown | 1038 S. Hill St. (bet. 11th St. & Olympic Blvd.) | 213-746-4287 | www.clubmayan.com

"Differing from the norm" Downtown, this "well-preserved" old theater done up to evoke a Mayan temple features "lots of different rooms and levels", most notably a "huge dance floor" where lessons precede "great live salsa bands" on Saturday nights; when it gets "hot 'n' heavy" in the "loud" hip-hop area, "darn-good drinks" cool the "friendly crowd" down.

McCabe's
18 | 14 | 18 | I

Santa Monica | 2455 Santa Monica Blvd. (bet. Chelsea Ave. & 25th St.) | 310-264-9704

"Comfy", "deep" sofas and "lots" of "big TVs" make this "no-frills" SaMo bar and grill "decorated with Scottish arms and tartans" "a sure-fire bet for the big game"; "solid pub food" helps to soak up the beer, while pool tables, shuffleboard and a "good jukebox" encourage couch potatoes to get up on their feet.

McCabe's Guitar Shop
23 | 16 | 18 | M

Santa Monica | 3101 Pico Blvd. (31st St.) | 310-828-4497 | www.mccabes.com

Now in its 40th year of performances at the rear of a SaMo instruments store, this "low-key" live-music venue attracts a "civil" crowd of "guitar purists" who don't mind sitting on metal chairs for "intimate" shows by "top-notch artists"; when there, do check out the "incredible museum" of "photos on the walls", but don't expect booze ("have a drink up the street before the show" if you like).

Medusa Lounge
∇ 19 | 21 | 18 | VE

Silver Lake | 3211 Beverly Blvd. (Dillon St.) | 213-382-5723 | www.medusaloungela.com

Originally a German restaurant built in ostensibly rococo style by a Hollywood set designer, this lounge on the outskirts of Silver Lake retains its predecessor's over-the-top mise-en-scène – whether you deem it "great" or "creepy", you certainly can't deny it's "quite an experience"; fittingly, nibbles and very pricey "drinks are of a unique variety", just like the "low-key", "cool" "crowd is eclectic."

Micky's   - | - | - | M

West Hollywood | 8857 Santa Monica Blvd. (San Vincente Blvd.) | 310-657-1176 | www.mickys.com

Closed after a 2007 fire, this high-energy, midpriced and low-drama gay restaurant/dance club in WeHo flames anew with revamped contempo decor (ostrich leather plays a part), a more open indoor/outdoor layout and the same old let-it-all-hang-out vibe; go-go boys, beefcake bartenders and poppy tunes go a long way toward promoting its hard-living dictum: 'drink triple, dance double, act single.'

Mint, The   21 | 14 | 18 | M

Mid-City | 6010 W. Pico Blvd. (Crescent Heights Blvd.) | 323-954-9400 | www.themintla.com

"LA's best unsigned bands" as well as (fingers crossed) "soon-to-be-famous bands from other cities" play this "perfect-sized venue" in Mid-City; musical genres include anything and everything (jazz, blues, country, Latin, folk, rock, etc.), and to accompany are "drinks that aren't watered down" and "decent food", "all at reasonable prices."

Mixville Bar at Edendale Grill   ▽ 25 | 27 | 22 | M

Silver Lake | 2838 Rowena Ave. (bet. Auburn & Rokeby Sts.) | 323-666-2000 | www.edendalegrill.com

"Catch up with friends" or "meet singles" at this "awesome" Silver Lake watering hole in a "cool", "old firehouse gone chic", where folks find no hassle grabbing "large and thoughtfully made martinis" and "nice wines" at the "long, user-friendly" bar; there's also a "great patio" for smoking, "lounging" and noshing on "interesting apps" under the stars.

Molly Malone's   19 | 15 | 19 | M

Fairfax | 575 S. Fairfax Ave. (6th St.) | 323-935-1577 | www.mollymalonesla.com

There's "lotsa music" at this Fairfax Irish "institution" that books up to three bands per night in its performance room; "soundproofing" means "you can't hear" the (usually) "loud, bracing rock" in the bar area, a boon to folks who just want to "hangout" amid the "traditional" decor and with a moderately priced pint of Guinness.

	APPEAL	DECOR	SERVICE	COST

Mood

20 | 21 | 18 | E

Hollywood | 6623 Hollywood Blvd. (Cherokee Ave.) | 323-464-6663 | www.moodla.com

Past its "heyday" by A-list standards, this Tinseltown dance club/ lounge with Balinese-inspired decor is "still pretty cool" for "showing off your grooves" via a "great variety of music" spun by "slick DJs"; the drinks are "a bit expensive", but they're "priced on par with the rest of Hollywood" and can be sipped in a "covered smoking area by the back bar."

Moonshadows

25 | 21 | 20 | E

Malibu | 20356 PCH (bet. Big Rock Dr. & Las Flores Mesa Dr.) | 310-456-3010 | www.moonshadowsmalibu.com

"If you want to see stars in Malibu (in the sky and from the movies)", come on up to this restaurant's "gorgeous" oceanside outdoor lounge where "beautiful sunsets" and "waves crashing on the rocky cliffs below" are also on view; a spot to "lounge, mix and mingle" with "upscale" "pretty people", the "mellow music" and usually "calm" vibe make it a "romantic-interlude" haven too – and while it's "expensive", "your date will be happy."

Mother Lode ⊅

14 | 9 | 17 | M

West Hollywood | 8944 Santa Monica Blvd. (Robertson Blvd.) | 310-659-9700

Gay men looking to escape the "expensive, sometimes-snobbish joints in WeHo" find "welcome relief" at this "beer-soaked" bar that "pumps the tunes", sports "average decor" and only takes cash; there's a "pool table if you're into that", but it's more known as a place to "meet nice people" "without a lot of pretentions" – and possibly hook up with a "one night stand."

Mountain Bar

∇ 19 | 18 | 17 | M

Chinatown | Central Plaza | 473 Gin Ling Way (bet. B'way & Hill St.) | 213-625-7500 | www.themountainbar.com

With an "unexpected" location in Chinatown's ornate Central Plaza, this lounge's "decent drinks" ("pricewise and tastewise"), "good DJs", dance floor and "roomy, well-decorated", red-heavy environs add up to one "well-balanced place to spend a couple of hours", especially "after gallery openings"; "occasionally, interesting lectures" and readings are also held.

| | APPEAL | DECOR | SERVICE | COST |

Musso & Frank Grill
23 | 20 | 23 | E

Hollywood | 6667 Hollywood Blvd. (bet. Cherokee & Las Palmas Aves.) |
323-467-7788 | www.mussoandfrankgrill.com

It's a hotbed of "tourists", but even Angelenos should stop in "once a
year" to toast this "ultimate Hollywood survivor" with "luscious libations" made by "crusty bartenders" and "superlatively served" by
"waiters as wonderfully snarky as they were 80 years ago"; the entire
endeavor, right down to "the old red-leather booths", "screams
nostalgia" – until the "not-cheap" check is brought.

NEW Must, The
- | - | - | M

Downtown | 118 W. Fifth St. (Spring St.) | 213-627-1162 |
www.themustbar.com

Downtown's rapidly gentrifying Historic Core welcomes this "great
new wine-and-beer bar" and lounge, which is especially popular during the nabe's well-attended Art Walk on the second Thursday of each
month; the emphasis for both food and drink is on affordability, while
the music's kept relatively low, making it convo-friendly for first-
daters and friends alike.

NEW MyHouse
∇ 25 | 23 | 16 | E

Hollywood | 7080 Hollywood Blvd. (La Brea Ave.) | 323-960-3300 |
www.myhousehollywood.com

"Don't waste your time stopping by if you're not on the list", because
"the bouncers won't give you the time of day" at this "'it' spot of the
moment" in Hollywood; fashioned to resemble a luxe mansion, the
"fabulous" experience includes a living room, a Miele appliance–filled
kitchen that functions as the main bar, a bedroom, a Jacuzzi-equipped
patio, "quality music", "beautiful people" and mortgage-sized tabs.

Nacional
20 | 19 | 17 | E

Hollywood | 1645 Wilcox Ave. (Hollywood Blvd.) | 323-962-7712 |
www.nacional.cc

Pre-Castro Cuba is the theme at this double-decker Hollywood
lounge, an "enjoyable location to meet friends or new people" while
imbibing mojitos and other pricey *bebidas* on cubist-inspired furniture;
fans say the second level with a fireplace and "open roof" is "reason
enough" to drop in, but folks wistful for its bygone days as an A-list
arena think it's "looking worn out."

Nic's Restaurant & Martini Lounge
22 | 21 | 21 | VE

Beverly Hills | 453 N. Cañon Dr. (Santa Monica Blvd.) | 310-550-5707 |
www.nicsbeverlyhills.com

"Excellent vibes" emanate from this "intimate" Beverly Hills resto-lounge that frames its New American fare and dozens of "creative", expensive martinis with "stylish", colorful vertical stripes and "soft lighting"; there's "live music some nights", but folks really "love the VodBox", a chilled room to shoot samples of the "fantastic" vodka.

⊠ Nine Thirty
23 | 26 | 21 | VE

Westwood | W Hotel | 930 Hilgard Ave. (Le Conte Ave.) | 310-443-8211 |
www.ninethirtyw.com

Summertime sipping at "the bar by the pool" can be a near-"perfect" experience at this W Hotel lounge in Westwood, but the "gorgeous", "elegant but still trendy" interior "draws a decent crowd" in its own right; indeed, it can get "pretty packed", especially on weekends, with folks who don't mind dropping "expensive" sums on "great" specialty drinks.

NoBAR
20 | 17 | 21 | M

North Hollywood | 10622 Magnolia Blvd. (Cahuenga Blvd.) | 818-753-0545 |
www.vintagebargroup.com

"In the middle of seemingly nowhere" NoHo, this "little" place to "chill" attracts "cool" locals who "really want to escape" (or have a surreptitious "tryst") via "quick, strong" moderately priced drinks and "decent music"; however, the "low-key" vibe repels excitement-seekers who say it "could be so much better with just a little personality."

Normandie Room
▽ 18 | 18 | 21 | E

West Hollywood | 8737 Santa Monica Blvd. (Hancock Ave.) | 310-659-6204 |
www.thenormandieroom.com

Boystown's boîte for "lipstick lesbians", this "tiny hangout" provides "chill-out fun" in the form of "a jukebox, pool table", trivia nights and more; it's such a "comfortable" neighborhood "standard", even those for whom it "doesn't have much appeal" admit it's "nice to know it's there."

O-Bar
21 | 23 | 21 | E

West Hollywood | 8279 Santa Monica Blvd. (Sweetzer Ave.) | 323-822-3300 |
www.obarla.com

New American fare is on the menu and "WeHo beef" is at the tables at this "pricey" eatery whose nightlife scene plays out at a "modern", "beautiful bar" and on a grassy patio – that is, when it's "crowded"; if you show up when it's "not very happening", look to the "kind, attentive bartenders" for company (but "bring a guy" if you're a girl – you might "get better service").

Oil Can Harry's ♥   ▽ 19 | 14 | 22 | E

Studio City | 11502 Ventura Blvd. (bet. Berry & Big Oak Drs.) | 818-760-9749 | www.oilcanharrysla.com

"Country is king" at this Studio City hoedown for members of "the GLBT crowd and those who love them", a "down-to-earth", "friendly" place to "go with friends" or "meet strangers" who "like to dance"; the Western tunes get folks two-stepping every night except Wednesday, when karaoke reigns, and Saturday, when disco takes over.

Opera   23 | 22 | 20 | E

Hollywood | 1650 Schrader Blvd. (Hollywood Blvd.) | 323-960-3300 | www.operahollywood.com

"If you're a dancer", this "beautiful", "trendy" Hollywood velvet-roper is "the place"; but if you're a "C-list celebrity hoping to make an appearance on another reality show", this isn't the right scene, as its "frequent" cameos on *The Hills* were so "last year" (nevertheless, the bouncers offer "no apologies for making you wait, rain or shine"); P.S. Crimson is its conjoined twin, and it's even "better" when they're "opened together."

Orchid, The   ▽ 19 | 19 | 15 | E

Koreatown | 607 S. Oxford Ave. (6th St.) | 213-251-8886 | www.orchidlosangeles.com

This massive two-story K-town club/eatery is notable for circa 100 pricey specialty martinis, fusiony nibbles, TVs for sports viewing and, most of all, 18 private karaoke rooms equipped with butler buttons for when guests need another round; the huge song catalog features not just tunes in English and Korean, but Chinese, Vietnamese, Indonesian and Tagalog as well.

Otheroom, The   22 | 21 | 18 | E

Venice | 1201 Abbot Kinney Blvd. (San Juan Ave.) | 310-396-6230

Though the "fab decor", "dim" "candlelight" and "packed" digs lend this lounge "an interesting East Coast feel" (there's a same-named NYC sibling), the "eclectic mix" of "laid-back", "hip" peeps who populate it are totally "representative of Venice"; it's beer, wine and champagne only, but the selection is "bountiful" – albeit "not cheap"; N.B. no food, but you can have it delivered from nearby restaurants.

Other Side, The

| - | - | - | M |

Silver Lake | 2538 Hyperion Ave. (Evans St.) | 323-661-4233 | www.flyingleapcafe.com

Even the very mature men who patronize this Silver Lake sing-along spot call it a "wrinkle room", but they also deem it "the only good gay piano bar left" on the Eastside, and a darn "friendly" one at that; boys who like show tunes and being "the youngest person by several decades" are sometimes also in attendance.

Parlor, The

| 20 | 18 | 18 | M |

Santa Monica | 1519 Wilshire Blvd. (15th St.) | 310-395-4139 | www.theparlorsm.com

"Everywhere you look", there's a TV at this "super-crowded", "super-loud" two-story "funhouse" in SaMo, so it's virtually guaranteed that whatever game the "backwards baseball cap and khakis"–wearing bros "want to see", it's tuned in somewhere; vying for attention is the "bevy of beauties who roll in nightly" to join in the "fried-finger-food" eating and "not-so-expensive" drinking.

☑ Peninsula Hotel Club Bar

| 26 | 26 | 25 | VE |

Beverly Hills | Peninsula Hotel Beverly Hills | 9882 S. Santa Monica Blvd. (Wilshire Blvd.) | 310-551-2888 | www.peninsula.com

"Moguls", "executives", "the rich and famous" and "silicone"-stuffed "gold diggers" make this "lavish", "elegant" Beverly Hills hotel "sophisticate" their "playground", canoodling by the "cozy fireplace" or ordering "excellent cocktails" from "top-notch" 'tenders at the "lovely" bar; of course, all this "class doesn't come cheap", "but at least you feel you are getting your money's worth."

Pete's Cafe & Bar

| 19 | 19 | 20 | M |

Downtown | 400 S. Main St. (4th St.) | 213-617-1000 | www.petescafe.com

"People-watching Downtown is always fun", and this "friendly", "old-time-feeling" New American restaurant with "windows all around" and a patio is a "delightful" choice to experience it; while it's "great for an after-work drink", later's even better, as it's one of the few places in the area you can "eat a real", moderately priced meal until 2 AM; N.B. try it on Tuesday when there's live jazz.

☑ Polo Lounge

27	25	26	VE

Beverly Hills | Beverly Hills Hotel | 9641 Sunset Blvd. (Crescent Dr.) | 310-887-2777 | www.beverlyhillshotel.com

"Pretend you're a movie star" and "be discreet" as you "survey for celebs" at this "cool and classy" "icon" in the Beverly Hills Hotel, a "stylish" indoor/outdoor environment for "nursing" an "amazing drink" or late-night supping to the strains of "mellow piano" or jazz courtesy of live musicians; "everything you've heard is true" about the "fabulous service" too, not to mention the "high prices" ("suck it up", it's "worth the experience").

Power House

▽ 24	11	19	I

Hollywood | 1714 N. Highland Ave. (Hollywood Blvd.) | 323-463-9438

Across the street from the gleaming Hollywood & Highland mall resides this "gritty dive""with darts, PBR on tap", other standard drinks that are "pretty cheap" "considering the area" and hipsters getting "happily wasted."

Prince, The

-	-	-	M

Koreatown | 3198 W. Seventh St. (New Hampshire Ave.) | 213-389-1586

Expect Hite beer, kimchi pancakes, "some of the best Korean-style fried chicken around" and throwback, non-ironic Brit decor at this subterranean K-town lounge; though both local businesspeople and hipsters deem it "a fun place to hang out", they usually keep to themselves in their red vinyl booths.

Rage

14	12	15	M

West Hollywood | 8911 Santa Monica Blvd. (San Vicente Blvd.) | 310-652-7055

If you're a "young and naive" gay boy, you might cheer this 18-and-over "WeHo mainstay" as an "awesome place to dance" with your "assorted hangers-on", especially since there are two floors on which to do so (hit the "small patio" for "relief from the roar" of the "hot crowd"); however, "once you hit 21", you might deem it "sleazy", "dated" and "so not the rage."

| | APPEAL | DECOR | SERVICE | COST |

Rainbow Bar & Grill
22 | 17 | 17 | M

West Hollywood | 9015 W. Sunset Blvd. (bet. Doheny Dr. & San Vicente Blvd.) | 310-278-4232 | www.rainbowbarandgrill.com

"Take a step back to the glory days of the Sunset Strip" when you enter this "relic of the hair-band era", where "on any random night you might spot" "some '80s rock star" "head banging" to a "killer" live act or ensconced in a big red booth with "fab pizza" from the "extensive, moderately priced menu"; "a few bars" serving "strong drinks" are scattered throughout the bi-level "maze", and "awesome memorabilia" abounds.

R Bar
▽ 24 | 23 | 23 | M

Koreatown | 3331 W. Eighth St. (Irolo St.) | 213-387-7227

"Love the feel of going to a secret club?" – "be sure to know" this "super-dark, intense" K-town dive's password (updated every couple of months on its MySpace page) to gain entry; "despite its hidden nature", it draws "lots of young folks" who get tanked on "great drinks for great prices", feed bills into a "jukebox full of rock" and pump fists for "some of the best unknown local bands."

Red Lion Tavern
22 | 18 | 18 | M

Silver Lake | 2366 Glendale Blvd. (Silver Lake Blvd.) | 323-662-5337 | www.redliontavern.net

"Bring on the lederhosen, bratwurst and beer!" – this "Bavarian retreat" in Silver Lake gets "boisterous" as the "young, feisty and ready to party" down "reasonably priced drinks" and "amazing" German eats; the "dark interior" often hosts a "snappy, witty piano player", but it's the rooftop biergarten that really "hops", especially during Oktoberfest.

Redwood Bar & Grill
18 | 18 | 19 | M

Downtown | 316 W. Second St. (bet. B'way & Hill St.) | 213-680-2600 | www.theredwoodbar.com

"Aaargh!", it's "pirate-themed awesomeness" at this "dark", "casual" Downtown bar and grill with sails, barrels, ropes, swords and "great booty" galore; even those who find the nauti-phernalia "a bit heavy-handed" declare it "a real place to drink" and eat the likes of beer-battered fish 'n' chips, plus there's the added attraction of live bands gigging on the small rear stage most evenings.

| | APPEAL | DECOR | SERVICE | COST |

Renee's Courtyard Café
20 | **19** | **18** | **M**

Santa Monica | 522 Wilshire Blvd. (bet. 5th & 6th Sts.) | 310-451-9341
The "timeless, thrown-together vibe" of this "cute, kitschy" bar/cafe in Santa Monica evokes everything from an "old French countryside cottage" to a "grandmother's parlor" to a "creepy doll" museum; many gravitate to the "nice outdoor space", but if you "don't appreciate having smoke blown" "from all sides", it might be best to stay inside and "explore" the "maze" of "nooks and corners."

Room, The
19 | **19** | **18** | **M**

Hollywood | 1626 N. Cahuenga Blvd. (bet. Hollywood Blvd. & Selma Ave.) | 323-462-7196
Santa Monica | 1323 Santa Monica Blvd. (bet. Euclid & 14th Sts.) | 310-458-0707
"So hidden", it may take you "an hour to find" them, these down-low dance halls with back-door entries are "worth the effort" if you're looking to "chill" with "a group friends or a date" amid "swanky" surroundings and "loud music"; N.B. the SaMo spot hosts comedy on Tuesday nights, while Hollywood sports a patio.

Roost, The ∅
∇ **19** | **16** | **21** | **I**

Atwater Village | 3100 Los Feliz Blvd. (Edenhurst Ave.) | 323-664-7272
The "best part" of this 80-year-old Atwater Village "hole-in-the-wall"? – "free popcorn!"; coming in second are "dirt-cheap" drinks, which you'll need cash to fund, so "be prepared."

Roosterfish ∅
∇ **18** | **11** | **18** | **M**

Venice | 1302 Abbot Kinney Blvd. (Cadiz Ct.) | 310-392-2123 | www.roosterfishbar.com
"Diversity is the rule" at this "no-frills", cash-only Venice gay joint that's "been there for years" and whose "friendly clientele" earns it a rep as "more down-to-earth than WeHo bars"; stay in the "run-down" interior if you're into "sleazy-fun" "decoupage", but head out to the patio if you need some fresh air and, on Sunday, BBQ'd burgers.

Roxy
20 | **15** | **15** | **E**

West Hollywood | 9009 W. Sunset Blvd. (bet. Doheny Dr. & San Vicente Blvd.) | 310-278-9457 | www.theroxyonsunset.com
"You'll find local acts, established artists and fun cover bands" at this "historic" "icon" of a live-music venue in West Hollywood; VIPs can re-

serve the "limited seating", but plebeians with general admission have to "stand" for the show (after clearing "too in-your-face security"), which makes it "not the most comfortable place" – on the upside, the "sightlines are good" since it's so "intimate."

Saddle Ranch

18	18	17	E

West Hollywood | 8371 W. Sunset Blvd. (bet. Crescent Heights & La Cienega Blvds.) | 323-656-2007
Universal City | Universal CityWalk | 1000 Universal Studios Blvd. (Buddy Holly Dr.) | 818-760-9680
www.srrestaurants.com

"Riding the mechanical bull is a ritual" for "young, wild" "out-of-towners", "drunk girls in thongs" and "reality stars" at these "over-the-top Western bars" on the Universal CityWalk and West Hollywood Strip; "gaudy", "cheesy" and "tourist-trappy", they're "always packed" with "rowdy" revelers downing "big, strong" drinks and "giant portions of mediocre" steakhouse vittles brought by "friendly", "fun" and "fame-hungry" staffers.

Saints & Sinners

18	18	19	M

Culver City | 10899 Venice Blvd. (bet. Overland & Sepulveda Aves.) | 310-842-8066

If you "ain't no saint", you'll "just love" this "small", heaven-meets-hell-themed Culver City bar with a "'70s, shagadelic vibe", "amazing fire pits", a back room for "making out" amid wallpaper depicting salacious scenes and "great cocktails" with libidinous monikers (and moderate price points to boot); "flame-blowing bartenders" "add to the appeal", and the crowd usually exudes that "rare" combination of "attitude with a sense of humor."

NEW Salute Wine Bar

-	-	-	E

Santa Monica | 2435 Main St. (Ocean Park Blvd.) | 310-450-3434 | www.salutewinebar.com

Santa Monicans salute this dimly lit wine lounge that feels like "someone's house party" – that is, if the home were equipped with a high-tech, "self-serve" dispensing system offering 2-oz. pours from the "decent", "fairly expensive" selection via prepaid cards; "get there early to get a seat" on one of the couches and order up a round of Italian small plates like bruschetta, salumi, cheeses, thin-crust pizza and desserts.

	APPEAL	DECOR	SERVICE	COST

Seven Grand
24 24 23 E

Downtown | 515 W. Seventh St., 2nd fl. (bet. Grand & Olive Sts.) | 213-614-0737 | www.sevengrand.la

Like an "urban hunting lodge" "styled to gentlemanly perfection", this "Downtown hideout" decked in "dark woods", "plaid" and "animal heads" is "the place to go for a whiskey and scotch education" administered by mixologists who "take exquisite care in crafting cocktails"; habitués include everyone from after-workers enjoying happy hour and "hipsters" playing pool to "college students" smoking on the "cool patio."

Sgt. Recruiter
- - - E

Los Feliz | 4655 Hollywood Blvd. (Vermont Ave.) | 323-669-3922

For "nice French wines" and "bistro basics" ("limited" but "well prepared"), Los Felizians enlist the services of this "cute", "Parisian"-style *bar à vin*; there's "only a few seats and not much standing room", but if you catch it on a "slow night", "you can linger" and get some "personalized attention" from the staff.

Short Stop
18 13 19 M

Echo Park | 1455 W. Sunset Blvd. (Sutherland St.) | 213-482-4942

"Cool but not too cool for school", this "awesome dive" in Echo Park is a "great place to dance the night away" to "hair metal, oldies, Latin and electro" or "learn to play pool"; despite all the "bumping", the vibe is "relaxed" because the "hipsters and hooligans" who populate it come "without attitude" – and the "drink prices aren't bad either."

⍓ Shutters Lobby Lounge
25 26 23 VE

Santa Monica | Shutters on the Beach | 1 Pico Blvd. (Ocean Ave.) | 310-458-0030 | www.shuttersonthebeach.com

"Drink in spectacular views of the Pacific", "movie stars" and, if you time it right, "one of the best sunsets" in SaMo at this "romantic" hotel lobby lounge whose "comfortable", "upscale", "beachy" style extends to a sandside deck; a live pianist helps to make it "an excellent place to unwind without much distraction" – but only "if you have the cash."

⍓ Sidebar
26 25 24 VE

Beverly Hills | Regent Beverly Wilshire Four Seasons Hotel | 9500 Wilshire Blvd. (El Camino Dr.) | 310-276-8500 | www.fourseasons.com

You "can't get any closer to the heart of Beverly Hills", both literally and figuratively, than at this minimalist, "*très* elegant" bar attached to

Wolfgang Puck's steakhouse, Cut, which is "always packed" with "schmoozing" "suits" and "tourists in overdone 'LA outfits'"; it's "expensive", but you can "feel good" about dropping big bucks, since "luxury service" comes with the package.

Side Door

| 23 | 22 | 20 | E |

Manhattan Beach | 900 Manhattan Ave. (bet. Bayview & Ocean Drs.) | 310-372-1684 | www.thesidedoor.org

"Tucked away from the frat scene" that can be Manhattan Beach, this "intimate" lounge foments a "VIP feel" with a "hiding place"–like locale, "amazing decor" and "blue mood lighting" to complement its "amazing martinis" and other "expensive", "interesting cocktails"; indeed, it can be "difficult to get in", so "go early to nab a sofa."

Silverlake Lounge ⊄

| ∇ 16 | 11 | 18 | M |

Silver Lake | 2906 Sunset Blvd. (Parkman Ave.) | 323-663-9636 | www.foldsilverlake.com

Check out the "latest up-and-coming indie rock bands" at this "cool neighborhood place" in Silver Lake, where "some great acts" take to the "tiny stage" almost every night of the week; the "hipsters" and "swingers" in the audience find it easy to brook the "kinda creepy" decor being that the prices are so reasonable.

⊠ Skybar

| 25 | 25 | 19 | VE |

West Hollywood | Mondrian Hotel | 8440 W. Sunset Blvd. (N. Olive Dr.) | 323-848-6025 | www.morganshotelgroup.com

Set in WeHo's Mondrian Hotel, this "original pool-bar scene" is "still going strong" with a "mesmerizing" pavilion for dancing and lounging and an "elegant wood deck" with an "illuminated pool", all backed by "fantastic views" of the city far below; a "star-studded", "otherworldly crowd" helps ensure that the "attitude" (not to mention the prices) remains "sky-high", so if you're not "recognizable", "go early before the velvet ropes" are snapped into place.

Social Hollywood

| 22 | 25 | 19 | VE |

Hollywood | 6525 W. Sunset Blvd. (Schrader Blvd.) | 323-462-5222 | www.citrusatsocial.com

"Get gussied up" for this "glamorous", "classy" compound (formerly the Hollywood Athletic Club) featuring "many different rooms and levels" to "relax on sofas" while sipping "extremely expensive" drinks or "boogie the night away" via an "incredible span of dance tunes"; even the on-premises Eclectic-French restaurant, Citrus, draws a "luscious crowd", and the staff exudes that "classic" Tinseltown "attitude."

Spaceland
22 | 15 | 18 | M

Silver Lake | 1717 Silver Lake Blvd. (Effie St.) | 323-661-4380 | www.clubspaceland.com

You could be "rocking out" to "some Icelandic band" fated for obscurity, an act "you'll hear next year on the radio" or a "well-known signed artist" at this "intimate", "respected" Silver Lake sound factory; the digs are "shabby" and you risk an "overdose of hipster irony", but on the upside, the "drinks are reasonably priced" and Monday night shows are free.

🆉 Standard, The (Downtown)
25 | 24 | 17 | E

Downtown | Standard Hotel | 550 S. Flower St. (6th St.) | 213-892-8080 | www.standardhotel.com

"Setting the standard" for Downtown destinations, this hotel rooftop "excels at views 'n' 'tude", with "energizing vistas, "beautiful", "trendy" patrons and "notoriously slow", sometimes "truculent" service; "moody music" spun by "fabulous DJs" fills the air both inside the red-and-white, "space-age" lounge and outside where "waterbed pods" flank the pool; "go on weeknights to avoid the long lines and steep cover", but "plan on spending a pretty penny" nonetheless.

Standard, The (Sunset)
21 | 22 | 18 | E

West Hollywood | Standard Hotel | 8300 W. Sunset Blvd. (Sweetzer Ave.) | 323-650-9090 | www.standardhotel.com

At this "posh", "modern", "surprisingly inviting" indoor/outdoor hotel lounge in WeHo, a "celebrity-gawking crowd" comes to "drink, listen to music and gab with their pals" while "laying by the pool" (it's a place to "relax", "not to let your hair down"); the "great views" are something to see, while the "expensive" "prices are what you'd expect for the Sunset Strip."

🆕 Stinkers
- | - | - | I

Silver Lake | 2939 W. Sunset Blvd. (Silver Lake Blvd.) | 323-661-6007 | www.stinkerstruckstop.com

Kitsch king Bobby Green (Bigfoot Lodge, Saints & Sinners) is the mind behind this irony-fueled yet warmhearted simulacrum of a small

1970s truck stop; Silver Lakers with the same tongue-in-cheek mindset "always have a good time" listening to rockabilly, guzzling "affordable" beers and noshing on Slim Jims and peanuts amid the 5,000 beer cans, Trans Am hood and mounted "skunk butts" that line the walls.

Stone Rose Lounge

| 24 | 24 | 21 | VE |

Crescent Heights | Sofitel Los Angeles | 8555 Beverly Blvd. (La Cienega Blvd.) | 310-228-6677 | www.gerberbars.com

Despite the "young, trendy, Hollywood crowd" that frequents it and the "model types" who provide the "amazing", "expensive" drinks, this "über-hip lounge" in Crescent Heights' Sofitel is surprisingly "pretention-free"; there's "plenty of seating" on "comfy couches" "if you arrive early", which you should since the "wonderful", fire-pit-warmed patio gets "packed", especially "on weekends."

NEW Suede

| - | - | - | M |

Downtown | Westin Bonaventure Hotel | 404 S. Figueroa St. (4th St.) | 213-489-3590 | www.suedebarla.com

The Downtown Financial District's famously cylindrical Westin Bonaventure houses this sleek and curvy, crimson-and-suede-heavy lobby spot offering free WiFi, a patio and a 4–8 PM weekday happy hour with $4 drinks and nibbles (other times, the libations remain reasonably priced); unsurprisingly, the early evening is a bustling tableau of fresh-off-the-clock office-workers, with hotel guests and local loft-dwellers moseying in after rush hour subsides and DJs start spinning.

Sunset Trocadero Lounge

| 20 | 19 | 20 | M |

West Hollywood | 8280 W. Sunset Blvd. (Sweetzer Ave.) | 323-656-7161

"An excellent alternative" to some of the less-intimate spots along the Sunset Strip, this "fun", "little" WeHo watering hole attracts a steady stream of revelers looking for a firm flow of "great drinks", especially from 6–8 PM daily when they're half off; style mavens who think the somewhat dark digs could "use a bit of a remodel" set themselves up on the "nice patio."

Teddy's

| 24 | 22 | 19 | VE |

Hollywood | Roosevelt Hotel | 7000 Hollywood Blvd. (Orange Dr.) | 323-466-7000 | www.thompsonhotels.com

"Classic LA" style is on display at this "classy", "retro"-looking lounge off the lobby of Hollywood's "beautiful", historic Roosevelt Hotel;

once past the velvet rope (the gatekeepers can be "a bit pretentious"), a "chic crowd" has "fun parading around" with tipples that are "worth the extra dollars", especially in light of "the atmosphere, music and company you get."

3rd Stop
21 | 18 | 20 | M

West Hollywood | 8636 W. Third St. (Williams Dr.) | 310-273-3605
Cedars-Sinai scrubs and "Hollywood assistants" get buzzed at this "charming", "casual" WeHo stop with a "tremendous selection" of "beers from all over", plus wine (the list "could use improvement") and "reasonably priced", "pretty good" bar food; sometimes it's a "low-key place to watch a game", other times (like happy hour) it's "loud" and "crowded", but "service is always snappy."

Three Clubs
19 | 14 | 22 | M

Hollywood | 1123 N. Vine St. (Santa Monica Blvd.) | 323-462-6441 | www.threeclubs.com
"Hard to find if you don't know what you're looking for", this "rock 'n' roll bar on the outskirts of Hollywood" with "no signage" employs "friendly bartenders" to pour "strong drinks" in "darker-than-night" digs; anyone and everyone "can get in" to shake it on the "crowded dance floor" or show the love to live acts such as bands, comedians and "smokin' burlesque" babes.

Tiki-Ti ⊄
25 | 24 | 23 | E

Los Feliz | 4427 W. Sunset Blvd. (bet. Fountain & Hillhurst Aves.) | 323-669-9381 | www.tiki-ti.com
"Bring a designated driver", because "two drinks and you're toast" at this longtime Los Feliz tiki bar whipping up "expensive but highly potent" tropical cocktails, most of its "own creation"; the space is "the size of a studio apartment", so "squeeze yourself in" and don't forget to bring cash; P.S. because it's "family-owned and -operated", "smoking is perfectly legal" when it's open – which seems "not too often" to some (the kinfolk take frequent vacations).

Tom Bergin's
22 | 19 | 22 | M

Fairfax | 840 S. Fairfax Ave. (bet. Olympic & Wilshire Blvds.) | 323-936-7151 | www.tombergins.com
"As traditional as an Irish pub can get", this "plain and simple" Fairfax "stomping ground" stars "darling bartenders from Dublin", "lots of

TVs", "filling fare" and rivers of Guinness at "good prices"; naturally, it's "crazy on St. Patty's Day", but "a lively crowd" can be found any time, as evidenced by all those shamrocks on the wall – each one "tells a story."

Tower Bar
23 | 25 | 21 | E

West Hollywood | Sunset Tower Hotel | 8358 W. Sunset Blvd. (bet. La Cienega Blvd. & Sweetzer Ave.) | 323-848-6677 | www.sunsettowerhotel.com

"For a mellow, sophisticated night" in WeHo, ascend to this "lovely, upscale" respite in the Sunset Tower Hotel, "tucked away" from the madness of the Strip; there's "usually a celebrity around", but its real "assets" are the views of the LA basin, the "polite staff" and the "excellent", sometimes "exotic", always expensive drinks.

Traxx
21 | 21 | 20 | E

Downtown | Union Station | 800 N. Alameda St. (bet. Cesar Chavez Ave. & Rte. 101) | 213-625-1999 | www.traxxrestaurant.com

"It's hard not to feel the romance" at this "throwback" resto-bar in Downtown's "timeless Union Station", a "gorgeous" structure imbued with Spanish Colonial, art deco and modern architectural features; whether you're "waiting for a train or have just arrived and need to un-wind", you'll feel like you're in a "glam" "'40s" "movie" as you "sip an old-school", "fairly high-priced" cocktail and "watch the world go by."

Tropicana Bar
23 | 22 | 16 | VE

Hollywood | Roosevelt Hotel | 7000 Hollywood Blvd. (Orange Dr.) | 323-466-7000 | www.thompsonhotels.com

"Feel like you're having a martini with Marilyn" at this "fantastic", "retro-hip" "hang" "surrounding the famed" David Hockney–designed pool at Hollywood's historic Roosevelt Hotel; true, it's "not quite" as hot as it was "a few years ago", but it's still a "cool venue" if you like "tons of girls in tight clothes" and don't mind a "pricey" check.

Troubadour
22 | 17 | 19 | M

West Hollywood | 9081 Santa Monica Blvd. (bet. Doheny Dr. & Robertson Blvd.) | 310-276-6168 | www.troubadour.com

"The world's best bands", those that are on the verge of "finding fame" and oldies that "still warm your heart" play this "fantastic venue" in WeHo that's "not too small", but "intimate" "enough that every spot is near the stage"; "liberally poured", midpriced drinks and food that'll "do in a pinch" are served, and while the decor's "outdated", the place is, after all, part of music "history."

Ultra Suede
18 | 15 | 17 | E

West Hollywood | 661 N. Robertson Blvd. (bet. Melrose Ave. & Santa Monica Blvd.) | 310-659-4551 | www.factorynightclub.com

"Go as your absolute most fabulous self" to this "compact" WeHo club that mainly attracts "gay twentysomething" males; never mind that the music's "sometimes great, sometimes tacky" and the decor could possibly benefit from a "serious overhaul" – as a place to "join up with friends for a night of dancing", it's "fun"; P.S. "girls who like girls" commandeer it on Fridays.

NEW Upper Manhattan Lounge
23 | 25 | 20 | E

Manhattan Beach | 3600 Highland Ave. (36th St.) | 310-545-2091 | www.uppermanhattanlounge.com

"A bit of Vegas in Manhattan Beach", this "upscale nightspot" requires its clientele – a "mix of young trendsetters and young-at-heart oldies" – to "dress up" for a "swanky" time fueled by "interesting" cocktails and "awesome food"; it's "a bit pricey", but you're also getting "fun entertainment like live bands" and "salacious song-and-dance" acts, after which "you can boogie on stage."

Vanguard
21 | 17 | 16 | E

Hollywood | 6021 Hollywood Blvd. (bet. Bronson Ave. & Gower St.) | 323-463-3331 | www.vanguardla.com

You'd be hard-pressed to find a more "spacious club" than this Hollywood "fail-safe" where "big spenders" "gyrate to the latest beats" on an "enormous dance floor" boasting an "incredible sound system"; the promoters really "pack the people" in, so if it gets too "crowded" and you can't gain entrée to the "awesome VIP lounge", take a breather on the "amazing patio."

NEW Varnish, The
- | - | - | E

Downtown | 118 E. Sixth St. (Main St.) | 213-622-9999 | www.thevarnishbar.com

Two NYC cocktail kingpins present this popular, tiny, wood-bedecked bar hidden behind a back door of the recently revamped Cole's restaurant in Downtown's Historic Core; piano players tickle the ivories, while bartenders, typically outfitted in throwback-wear, specialize in mixers that are retro-minded in every way but the price.

Velvet Margarita Cantina

| 21 | 24 | 20 | E |

Hollywood | 1612 N. Cahuenga Blvd. (bet. Hollywood Blvd. & Selma Ave.) | 323-469-2000 | www.velvetmargarita.com

If "Tijuana" had a "Disneyland", it might look like this "wonderfully kitschy" Hollywood cantina festooned with "blue velvet, sombreros tacked to the ceiling", a "Speedy Gonzalez" painting, "out-there images on the TV screen" and lots more "gaudy-fun" elements; the "festive" atmosphere is bolstered by "great margaritas" and over 100 tequilas including "brands you may never have heard of."

Veranda Bar

| - | - | - | E |

Downtown | Figueroa Hotel | 939 S. Figueroa St. (Olympic Blvd.) | 213-627-8971 | www.figueroahotel.com

Downtown LA meets Marrakech at this "Moroccan-themed" pool-adjacent lounge in the Figueroa Hotel, where tiled tabletops, fountains and indigenous fabrics are the eye-poppers in the "well-done" design scheme; after-workers, loft-dwellers and LA Live-ticket-holders say the pricey mojitos are "best at sunset."

Verdugo Bar

| - | - | - | M |

Glassell Park | 3408 Verdugo Rd. (W. Ave. 34) | 323-257-3408 | www.verdugobar.com

Glassell Park gets its own classy hipster hang with this "up-and-coming spot" in a "shady" stretch of the nigh gentrifying 'hood; a "knowledgeable staff" administers the "amazing beer selection", which can be sampled at the curvy, art deco-inspired bar, in leather booths or on the rear patio.

☑ Vibrato Grill & Jazz

| 25 | 26 | 25 | VE |

Bel-Air | 2930 N. Beverly Glen Circle (N. Beverly Glen Blvd.) | 310-474-9400 | www.vibratogrilljazz.com

"Don't be fooled" by its location in an "out-of-the-way" Bel-Air "strip mall", because this "mellow" supper club boasts a "stunning" interior design, a "terrific wine list" and "yummy food" – and with famed trumpeter "Herb Alpert at the helm, you know" the live jazz will be "exceptional" and the talent "world-class"; you'll "pay heavily", but it's "worth it" for a "great night" of "romance."

	APPEAL	DECOR	SERVICE	COST

Vice

| | - | - | - | E |

Hollywood | 6364 Hollywood Blvd. (Cahuenga Blvd.) | 323-462-7827 |
www.vicehollywood.com

"An array of Hollywood Boulevard fixtures" succumbs to its vices at
this "edgy", "minimal", "intimate" lounge where a "narrow passage-
way" (set up like a "catwalk") flanked by bottle-served tables and a
bar "opens up" to a "small dance floor", which resides under a "cute
little VIP area"; "groovy music" and "attentive" staffers do their part
to abet the debauchery.

Villa

| | ▽ 20 | 20 | 16 | VE |

West Hollywood | 8623 Melrose Ave. (Huntley Dr.) | 310-289-8623 |
www.villalounge.com

"Rude doormen" "make you wait unless you're A-list" at this
rollicking West Hollywood haunt that comes "complete with celebrities", their agents, stylists and hangers-on, plus "*TMZ*" and other
"paparazzi"; strewn with "awesome", "mismatched decor", the interior's about "the size of your living room", while the tabs can run as
high as your rent.

Viper Room

| | 19 | 15 | 16 | E |

West Hollywood | 8852 W. Sunset Blvd. (Larrabee St.) | 310-358-1880 |
www.viperroom.com

"Famous bands perform secret" "up-close, in-your-face" shows while
"up-and-comers" prey upon "music-business heavy hitters" at this
"infamous" WeHo "heat box" that's as "seedy", "dinky", "dark and
loud" as it "should be"; but over-it types dis that "1992 called" and "it
wants its grunge vibe back" from the "overpriced sham."

Well, The

| | 19 | 16 | 20 | M |

Hollywood | 6255 W. Sunset Blvd. (bet. Argyle Ave. & Vine St.) |
323-467-9355

Its entrance is "hidden on a side street" (Argyle Avenue), "so look
carefully" to find this "low-lit" lounge promising a "friendly, fast staff",
"one of the better jukeboxes around" and a "lack of Hollywood preten-
tion"; "hotties" start arriving for the "great happy hour" – when the
"strong, well-made drinks" and apps are even more "decently
priced" – and usually stick around the "square-shaped bar" late
into the evening.

Whiskey Blue

22 | 23 | 21 | VE

Westwood | W Hotel | 930 Hilgard Ave. (Le Conte Ave.) | 310-208-8765 | www.gerberbars.com

On many evenings, "lots of beautiful people" "chill" at this "sleek", "velvet-rope kind of place" in the W Hotel situated on a "quiet" swath of Westwood – and during most happy hours, it's an out-and-out "meat market", with an "after-work crowd" lounging on "comfortable couches" or bellying up to the "long bar" for "expensive", "fun cocktails"; however, on some nights there may be no one in sight save "suits staying the night."

Whisky A Go-Go

21 | 15 | 17 | E

West Hollywood | 8901 W. Sunset Blvd. (bet. Clark St. & San Vicente Blvd.) | 310-652-4202 | www.whiskyagogo.com

"An oldie but goodie" cheer fans of this "loud, proud", "historic" live music venue in WeHo, where "new artists" test their mettle and "some of your favorites may even make an appearance"; but it's just "living off its name" carp critics who complain of only "occasional good shows" ("too many 14-year-old rock-star wannabes") and digs that have "seen better days."

Windows Lounge

∇ 25 | 27 | 24 | VE

Beverly Hills | Four Seasons Hotel | 300 S. Doheny Dr. (Burton Way) | 310-273-2222 | www.fourseasons.com

Hobnob with "athletes, celebs and models" at this "elegant" indoor/outdoor lounge inside the "fantastic" Four Seasons in Beverly Hills; "friendly service" is commensurate with the "expensive" tabs, which also pay for entertainment such as a DJ spinning on Wednesday and live music Thursday–Sunday.

Winstons

20 | 19 | 19 | E

West Hollywood | 7746 Santa Monica Blvd. (bet. Genesee & Spaulding Aves.) | 323-654-0105 | www.winstonsla.com

If "you go where the crowds" are, you've undoubtedly squeezed into this "small, dark" WeHo watering hole whose strip of banquettes – accompanied by ottomans, tables and chairs done up in rich browns – gets "packed" "quickly" with "young", "dressed-up" Industry types; indeed, there's "so much drama" getting in, you may want to "pop a Xanax" beforehand.

	APPEAL	DECOR	SERVICE	COST

Woods, The
▽ 20 | 24 | 21 | M

Hollywood | 1533 N. La Brea Ave. (Sunset Blvd.) | 323-876-6612 | www.vintagebargroup.com

"Despite its strip-mall locale", Holly-woodsmen and their ladies "dig" this "comfy, cozy" bar with a sleekly interpreted "hunting-lodge" theme (antler chandeliers, lumber walls, tree-stump tables); "mean martinis" and such at moderate prices plus "wonderful music that makes you want to move" keep it "tightly packed" with a "crowd gone wild."

World Cafe
20 | 20 | 18 | E

Santa Monica | 2820 Main St. (Ashland Ave.) | 310-392-1661 | www.worldcafela.com

"Take a date" or "mingle" with "singles" at this "laid-back" Santa Monica restaurant where you can "sit at the bar, in the lounge" or on the "large patio"; "mean mojitos" and "fun decor" make you "feel like you've ventured around the world", and though some sniff the experience is "a little dull" and "overpriced", "great happy-hour deals" bring back the excitement.

X Bar
20 | 23 | 19 | VE

Century City | Hyatt Regency Century Plaza | 2025 Ave. of the Stars (Constellation Blvd.) | 310-228-1234 | www.xbarla.com

The "hippest" spot in Century City by default ("there's not much else going on"), this Hyatt Regency lounge draws "CAA" "professionals" as well as "conference people" staying at the hotel; sporting "modern decor" and private booths inside and a fire pit on the "huge patio", it "attempts a clubby feel" with "good DJs" "when night falls" and "costly" cocktails (no worries, "you get what you pay for").

Ye Rustic Inn
18 | 11 | 20 | M

Los Feliz | 1831 Hillhurst Ave. (bet. Melbourne & Russell Aves.) | 323-662-5757

"Sassy bartenders" dole out "stiff drinks" and "great wings" "with a side of awesome" at this "low-key" Los Feliz dive filled with "lots of TVs" and a "fabulous" jukebox; it's "great for a drink in the afternoon" and Bloody Mary breakfasts Friday–Sunday – in fact, you "could kill a whole day here", especially since it's so "dark", "you never know what time it is."

	APPEAL	DECOR	SERVICE	COST

York, The

23 | 23 | 24 | M

Highland Park | 5018 York Blvd. (N. Ave. 50) | 323-255-9675 |
www.theyorkonyork.com

An "unexpectedly hip scene" for Highland Park, this "fantastic", "loft-like" gastropub proffers a "great selection of unique beers" alongside "scrumptious food"; though it's "big", it "fills up nicely" with an "interesting" "mix" of folks who order from "knowledgeable" staffers after studying the chalkboard "menus on the wall" ("avoid the tables in front of them unless you want people standing over you all night").

Zanzibar

20 | 19 | 18 | E

Santa Monica | 1301 Fifth St. (Arizona Ave.) | 310-451-2221 |
www.zanzibarlive.com

"Small enough to seem intimate" yet "large enough to be fun", this perpetually "packed" Santa Monica lounge sets a "moody" tone with "exotic decor" and DJs who tote an "eclectic" "library" of "house", "hip-hop", "salsa", "Afro-funk", whatever; the "diverse" clientele's cool dance-floor "grooves" make for "hot nights" – literally, "it never feels like there's any a/c in the place."

Zinc Lounge

22 | 20 | 20 | E

Manhattan Beach | Shade Hotel | 1221 N. Valley Dr. (Manhattan Beach Blvd.) |
310-546-4995 | www.shadehotel.com

Like a "high-end" "Hollywood" happening in Manhattan Beach, this lounge in the Shade Hotel provides a "place to see and be seen" for local "trendy, hip women", "flashy, cool men" and "cougars on the prowl"; everyone "dresses up" to blend in with the chic, modern furnishings inside and on the terrace.

Locations

Includes venue names and Appeal ratings.

LA Central

ATWATER VILLAGE

Bigfoot Lodge	23
Griffin	23
Roost	19

CHINATOWN

Grand Star Jazz	20
Hop Louie	18
Mountain Bar	19

CRESCENT HEIGHTS

El Carmen	20
Guy's	24
Stone Rose	24

DOWNTOWN

Z NEW Association	27
Bar 107	21
Bonaventure	19
Bordello	22
Broadway Bar	21
Casey's	20
NEW Club Nokia	23
NEW Conga Room	21
NEW Corkbar	-
NEW Crocker Club	-
Z Edison Lounge	26
Elevate Lounge	23
Gallery Bar	-
Golden Gopher	22
King Edward Saloon	-
NEW Lab	-
La Cita	19

Library Bar	22
Mayan	19
NEW Must	-
Pete's	19
Redwood	18
Seven Grand	24
Z Standard (Downtown)	25
NEW Suede	-
Traxx	21
NEW Varnish	-
Veranda	-

ECHO PARK

Echo/Echoplex	22
Gold Room	-
Little Joy	21
Short Stop	18

FAIRFAX

Dime	19
Insomnia	20
Molly Malone's	19
Tom Bergin's	22

GLASSELL PARK

Verdugo	-

HIGHLAND PARK

Footsie's	-
York	23

HOLLYWOOD

Avalon	20
Bar	-
NEW Bar Delux	19

NEW Bardot	21	Teddy's	24
Beauty Bar	17	Three Clubs	19
Boardner's	21	Tropicana	23
Boulevard 3	23	Vanguard	21
Burgundy Room	22	Velvet Margarita	21
Cabana Club	20	Vice	-
Catalina Jazz	22	Well	19
Cat & Fiddle	22	Woods	20
Central	-		

KOREATOWN

Coach & Horses	21	Brass Monkey	20
Crimson	23	Frank 'n Hank	-
NEW Ecco	19	HMS Bounty	22
Falcon	21	Orchid	19
Frolic Room	22	Prince	-
Green Door	20	R Bar	24
NEW Halo	-		

LEIMERT PARK

Happy Ending	-	Babe's & Ricky's	-
Hollywood Billiards	19		

LINCOLN HEIGHTS

Hollywood Canteen	18	Airliner	18
Hotel Café	25		

LOS FELIZ

NEW h.wood	-	NEW Cuba Libre	23
Jimmy's	22	Drawing Room	19
Jumbo's	21	Dresden Room	23
King King	22	Good Luck Bar	21
NEW Kitchen 24	-	Sgt. Recruiter	-
Knitting Factory	19	Tiki-Ti	25
Laugh Factory	21	Ye Rustic Inn	18
LAX	21		

MELROSE

Les Deux	23	Bungalow Club	20
Lou	23	Improv	22
L Scorpion	21		

Mood	20		
Musso & Frank	23		

MID-CITY

NEW MyHouse	25	Café-Club	22
Nacional	20	Mint	21
Opera	23		
Power House	24		
Room	19		
Social H'wood	22		

Menus, photos, voting and more – free at ZAGAT.com

MID-WILSHIRE

El Rey Theatre	23
Little Bar	-

PICO-ROBERTSON

Joint	16

SILVER LAKE

Akbar	19
NEW Barbarella	-
Cha Cha Lounge	19
Eagle LA	25
El Cid	20
Faultline	26
4100 Bar	21
Intelligentsia	21
LAMILL	23
Little Temple	18
Medusa	19
Mixville	25
Other Side	-
Red Lion	22
Silverlake	16
Spaceland	22
NEW Stinkers	-

WEST HOLLYWOOD

Z Abbey	23
NEW ADCB	22
NEW Apple	-
Area	19
Z Asia de Cuba	24
Bar Lubitsch	21
Z Bar Marmont	26
Z Barney's Beanery	18
Belmont	19
Z Chateau Marmont	26
Coco de Ville	24
Comedy Store	20
NEW Crown Bar	22

East/West	21
Eleven	21
Formosa Café	20
Foxtail	23
Fubar	18
here	19
Z Hse. of Blues	22
Hyde Lounge	23
Key Club	19
Largo	19
Micky's	-
Mother Lode	14
Normandie	18
O-Bar	21
Rage	14
Rainbow	22
Roxy	20
Saddle Ranch	18
Z Skybar	25
Standard (Sunset)	21
Sunset Trocadero	20
3rd Stop	21
Tower Bar	23
Troubadour	22
Ultra Suede	18
Villa	20
Viper Room	19
Whisky A Go-Go	21
Winstons	20

LA West

BEL-AIR

Z Hotel Bel-Air	27
Z Vibrato	25

BEVERLY HILLS

Bar NINETEEN12	23
Bar Noir	24

LOCATIONS

🔲 Mastro's Steak	26
Nic's	22
🔲 Peninsula	26
🔲 Polo Lounge	27
🔲 Sidebar	26
Windows Lounge	25

CENTURY CITY

X Bar	20

CULVER CITY

Alibi Room	18
BottleRock	20
🔲 Father's Office	23
Mandrake	21
Saints & Sinners	18

MALIBU

Moonshadows	25

SANTA MONICA

Air Conditioned	19
Barcopa	18
Bodega Wine	22
Cameo Bar	25
Chloe	23
Cock 'n Bull	19
NEW Copa d'Oro	21
Daily Pint	18
NEW Dakota	22
🔲 Father's Office	23
Harvelle's	23
Hideout	17
Library Ale	22
McCabe's	18
McCabe's Guitar	23
Parlor	20
Renee's	20
Room	19
NEW Salute Wine	-

🔲 Shutters	25
World Cafe	20
Zanzibar	20

VENICE

Air Conditioned	19
Brig	18
Garter	17
Hal's	22
Otheroom	22
Roosterfish	18

WEST LA

Arsenal	19
Del's Saloon	16
Liquid Kitty	19

WESTWOOD

Gypsy Café	18
🔲 Nine Thirty	23
Whiskey Blue	22

South Bay

LONG BEACH

Cohiba	18
Library Coffee	22

MANHATTAN BEACH

Ercole's	20
Side Door	23
NEW Upper Manhattan	23
Zinc	22

REDONDO BEACH

Bull Pen	17

Pasadena & Environs

EAGLE ROCK

Chalet	22

PASADENA

Bodega Wine	22
Z Langham Huntington	25
Lucky Baldwins	20

San Fernando Valley

NORTH HOLLYWOOD

Match	-
NoBAR	20

STUDIO CITY

Baked Potato	19
Clear	15
Firefly	24

NEW Laurel Tavern	25
Mama Juana's	-
Oil Can Harry's	19

UNIVERSAL CITY

Saddle Ranch	18

VALLEY VILLAGE

NEW Fifth	-

Conejo Valley

AGOURA HILLS

Canyon Club	19

LOCATIONS

Special Appeals

Listings cover the best in each category and include venue names, locations and Appeal ratings. Multi-location nightspots' features may vary by branch.

AFTER WORK

Belmont | **W Hollywood**	19
Bonaventure | **Downtown**	19
Broadway Bar | **Downtown**	21
Casey's | **Downtown**	20
NEW Copa d'Oro | **Santa Monica**	21
NEW Corkbar | **Downtown**	-
NEW Crocker Club | **Downtown**	-
El Carmen | **Crescent Hts**	20
Firefly | **Studio City**	24
Gallery Bar | **Downtown**	-
Golden Gopher | **Downtown**	22
Library Bar | **Downtown**	22
Little Bar | **Mid-Wilshire**	-
Lou | **Hollywood**	23
Match | **N Hollywood**	-
NEW Must | **Downtown**	-
Pete's | **Downtown**	19
Seven Grand | **Downtown**	24
Z Standard (Downtown) | **Downtown**	25
NEW Stinkers | **Silver Lake**	-
NEW Suede | **Downtown**	-
Traxx | **Downtown**	21
Veranda | **Downtown**	-
Well | **Hollywood**	19
Whiskey Blue | **Westwood**	22
Windows Lounge | **Beverly Hills**	25

BLUES

Babe's & Ricky's | **Leimert Pk**	-
Café-Club | **Mid-City**	22
NEW Dakota | **Santa Monica**	22

Z Edison Lounge | **Downtown**	26
Z Hse. of Blues | **W Hollywood**	22
Z Langham Huntington | **Pasadena**	25
Mint | **Mid-City**	21

CELEB-SIGHTINGS

NEW Apple | **W Hollywood**	-
Z Asia de Cuba | **W Hollywood**	24
NEW Bar Delux | **Hollywood**	19
NEW Bardot | **Hollywood**	21
Z Bar Marmont | **W Hollywood**	26
Bar Noir | **Beverly Hills**	24
Cameo Bar | **Santa Monica**	25
Z Chateau Marmont | **W Hollywood**	26
Coco de Ville | **W Hollywood**	24
NEW Conga Room | **Downtown**	21
NEW Crown Bar | **W Hollywood**	22
Falcon | **Hollywood**	21
Foxtail | **W Hollywood**	23
Green Door | **Hollywood**	20
Guy's | **Crescent Hts**	24
NEW Halo | **Hollywood**	-
NEW h.wood | **Hollywood**	-
Hyde Lounge | **W Hollywood**	23
Les Deux | **Hollywood**	23
Z Mastro's Steak | **Beverly Hills**	26
Moonshadows | **Malibu**	25
NEW MyHouse | **Hollywood**	25
Z Nine Thirty | **Westwood**	23
Z Polo Lounge | **Beverly Hills**	27
Rainbow | **W Hollywood**	22

Menus, photos, voting and more – free at ZAGAT.com

✓ Shutters | **Santa Monica**	25
✓ Skybar | **W Hollywood**	25
Social H'wood | **Hollywood**	22
Standard (Sunset) | **W Hollywood**	21
✓ Standard (Downtown) | **Downtown**	25
Stone Rose | **Crescent Hts**	24
Teddy's | **Hollywood**	24
Tower Bar | **W Hollywood**	23
Tropicana | **Hollywood**	23
Villa | **W Hollywood**	20
Windows Lounge | **Beverly Hills**	25
Winstons | **W Hollywood**	20
X Bar | **Century City**	20

COFFEEHOUSES

Insomnia | **Fairfax**	20
Intelligentsia | **Silver Lake**	21
LAMILL | **Silver Lake**	23
Library Coffee | **Long Bch**	22

COMEDY CLUBS

(Call ahead to check nights, times, acts and covers)

Comedy Store | **W Hollywood**	20
Improv | **Melrose**	22
Laugh Factory | **Hollywood**	21

DANCING

✓ Abbey | **W Hollywood**	23
Air Conditioned | **Venice**	19
Airliner | **Lincoln Hts**	18
Akbar | **Silver Lake**	19
Area | **W Hollywood**	19
Avalon | **Hollywood**	20
NEW Barbarella | **Silver Lake**	-
Barcopa | **Santa Monica**	18
NEW Bardot | **Hollywood**	21
Bar Lubitsch | **W Hollywood**	21
Bar 107 | **Downtown**	21

Beauty Bar | **Hollywood**	17
Boardner's | **Hollywood**	21
Boulevard 3 | **Hollywood**	23
Bull Pen | **Redondo Bch**	17
Bungalow Club | **Melrose**	20
Cabana Club | **Hollywood**	20
Café-Club | **Mid-City**	22
Canyon Club | **Agoura Hills**	19
Casey's | **Downtown**	20
Central | **Hollywood**	-
Clear | **Studio City**	15
Cock 'n Bull | **Santa Monica**	19
Coco de Ville | **W Hollywood**	24
Cohiba | **Long Bch**	18
NEW Conga Room | **Downtown**	21
Crimson | **Hollywood**	23
NEW Crown Bar | **W Hollywood**	22
NEW Cuba Libre | **Los Feliz**	23
Dime | **Fairfax**	19
NEW Ecco | **Hollywood**	19
✓ Edison Lounge | **Downtown**	26
El Cid | **Silver Lake**	20
Elevate Lounge | **Downtown**	23
Eleven | **W Hollywood**	21
Foxtail | **W Hollywood**	23
Fubar | **W Hollywood**	18
Garter | **Venice**	17
Grand Star Jazz | **Chinatown**	20
Green Door | **Hollywood**	20
Guy's | **Crescent Hts**	24
Gypsy Café | **Westwood**	18
NEW Halo | **Hollywood**	-
here | **W Hollywood**	19
Hideout | **Santa Monica**	17
Hollywood Canteen | **Hollywood**	18
Jimmy's | **Hollywood**	22
King King | **Hollywood**	22
La Cita | **Downtown**	19
LAX | **Hollywood**	21

SPECIAL APPEALS

Les Deux | **Hollywood**	23	Café-Club | **Mid-City**	22
Little Temple | **Silver Lake**	18	Cha Cha Lounge | **Silver Lake**	19
Mama Juana's | **Studio City**	-	Coach & Horses | **Hollywood**	21
Mayan | **Downtown**	19	Daily Pint | **Santa Monica**	18
Medusa | **Silver Lake**	19	Del's Saloon | **West LA**	16
Micky's | **W Hollywood**	-	Dime | **Fairfax**	19
Mood | **Hollywood**	20	Drawing Room | **Los Feliz**	19
Mountain Bar | **Chinatown**	19	Ercole's | **Manhattan Bch**	20
NEW MyHouse | **Hollywood**	25	Faultline | **Silver Lake**	26
Nacional | **Hollywood**	20	Footsie's | **Highland Pk**	-
Oil Can Harry's | **Studio City**	19	Frank 'n Hank | **Koreatown**	-
Opera | **Hollywood**	23	Frolic Room | **Hollywood**	22
Orchid | **Koreatown**	19	Fubar | **W Hollywood**	18
Rage | **W Hollywood**	14	Gold Room | **Echo Pk**	-
Rainbow | **W Hollywood**	22	HMS Bounty | **Koreatown**	22
Room | **multi.**	19	Hop Louie | **Chinatown**	18
Roxy | **W Hollywood**	20	Jumbo's | **Hollywood**	21
Saddle Ranch | **W Hollywood**	18	King Edward Saloon | **Downtown**	-
Short Stop | **Echo Pk**	18	La Cita | **Downtown**	19
Z Skybar | **W Hollywood**	25	Liquid Kitty | **West LA**	19
Social H'wood | **Hollywood**	22	Little Bar | **Mid-Wilshire**	-
Z Standard (Downtown) | **Downtown**	25	Little Joy | **Echo Pk**	21
		Lucky Baldwins | **Pasadena**	20
Three Clubs | **Hollywood**	19	Mother Lode | **W Hollywood**	14
Ultra Suede | **W Hollywood**	18	Power House | **Hollywood**	24
NEW Upper Manhattan | **Manhattan Bch**	23	Prince | **Koreatown**	-
		R Bar | **Koreatown**	24
Vanguard | **Hollywood**	21	Roost | **Atwater Vill**	19
Vice | **Hollywood**	-	Short Stop | **Echo Pk**	18
Winstons | **W Hollywood**	20	Ye Rustic Inn | **Los Feliz**	18
Zanzibar | **Santa Monica**	20		

DIVES

Arsenal | **West LA**	19
Z Barney's Beanery | **W Hollywood**	18
Bar 107 | **Downtown**	21
Boardner's | **Hollywood**	21
Brig | **Venice**	18
Burgundy Room | **Hollywood**	22

DRINK SPECIALISTS

BEER
(* Microbrewery)

Alibi Room | **Culver City**	18
NEW Barbarella | **Silver Lake**	-
Z Barney's Beanery | **W Hollywood**	18
Bonaventure* | **Downtown**	19

Cat & Fiddle	Hollywood	22
Cock 'n Bull	Santa Monica	19
Daily Pint	Santa Monica	18
Dime	Fairfax	19
Z Father's Office	multi.	23
NEW Lab	Downtown	-
NEW Laurel Tavern	Studio City	25
Library Ale	Santa Monica	22
Library Bar	Downtown	22
Lucky Baldwins	Pasadena	20
Otheroom	Venice	22
Red Lion	Silver Lake	22
Redwood	Downtown	18
3rd Stop	W Hollywood	21
Verdugo	Glassell Pk	-
York	Highland Pk	23

CHAMPAGNE

Z Hotel Bel-Air	Bel-Air	27
Z Langham Huntington	Pasadena	25
Z Mastro's Steak	Beverly Hills	26
Z Nine Thirty	Westwood	23
Otheroom	Venice	22
Z Peninsula	Beverly Hills	26
Z Polo Lounge	Beverly Hills	27
Z Shutters	Santa Monica	25
Tower Bar	W Hollywood	23
Windows Lounge	Beverly Hills	25

COCKTAILS

Z Abbey	W Hollywood	23
NEW ADCB	W Hollywood	22
Arsenal	West LA	19
Z Asia de Cuba	W Hollywood	24
Z NEW Association	Downtown	27
Avalon	Hollywood	20
Bar	Hollywood	-
NEW Bar Delux	Hollywood	19
Z Bar Marmont	W Hollywood	26

Bar Noir	Beverly Hills	24
Belmont	W Hollywood	19
Brig	Venice	18
Cameo Bar	Santa Monica	25
Z Chateau Marmont	W Hollywood	26
Chloe	Santa Monica	23
NEW Copa d'Oro	Santa Monica	21
NEW Crocker Club	Downtown	-
Falcon	Hollywood	21
Formosa Café	W Hollywood	20
Gallery Bar	Downtown	-
Z Hotel Bel-Air	Bel-Air	27
NEW Lab	Downtown	-
Match	N Hollywood	-
Mixville	Silver Lake	25
Musso & Frank	Hollywood	23
Nacional	Hollywood	20
Z Nine Thirty	Westwood	23
Z Peninsula	Beverly Hills	26
Saints & Sinners	Culver City	18
Seven Grand	Downtown	24
Social H'wood	Hollywood	22
Tiki-Ti	Los Feliz	25
Tower Bar	W Hollywood	23
Tropicana	Hollywood	23
NEW Varnish	Downtown	-
Well	Hollywood	19
World Cafe	Santa Monica	20
Zinc	Manhattan Bch	22

MARTINIS

Z Abbey	W Hollywood	23
Arsenal	West LA	19
Z Asia de Cuba	W Hollywood	24
Avalon	Hollywood	20
Barcopa	Santa Monica	18
Z Bar Marmont	W Hollywood	26
Bar Noir	Beverly Hills	24
Brig	Venice	18

Cameo Bar | **Santa Monica**	25
🗹 Chateau Marmont | **W Hollywood**	26
Gallery Bar | **Downtown**	-
Golden Gopher | **Downtown**	22
Hal's | **Venice**	22
🗹 Hotel Bel-Air | **Bel-Air**	27
Liquid Kitty | **West LA**	19
🗹 Mastro's Steak | **Beverly Hills**	26
Mixville | **Silver Lake**	25
Nic's | **Beverly Hills**	22
🗹 Nine Thirty | **Westwood**	23
Orchid | **Koreatown**	19
🗹 Polo Lounge | **Beverly Hills**	27
Room | **multi.**	19
🗹 Shutters | **Santa Monica**	25
Side Door | **Manhattan Bch**	23
Sunset Trocadero | **W Hollywood**	20
Three Clubs | **Hollywood**	19
Tower Bar | **W Hollywood**	23
Traxx | **Downtown**	21
NEW Upper Manhattan | **Manhattan Bch**	23
NEW Varnish | **Downtown**	-
🗹 Vibrato | **Bel-Air**	25
Windows Lounge | **Beverly Hills**	25

SAKE/SHOCHU/SOJU

Little Bar | **Mid-Wilshire**	-

SCOTCH/SINGLE MALTS

Bar Noir | **Beverly Hills**	24
Belmont | **W Hollywood**	19
🗹 Chateau Marmont | **W Hollywood**	26
Daily Pint | **Santa Monica**	18
Gallery Bar | **Downtown**	-
🗹 Hotel Bel-Air | **Bel-Air**	27
King King | **Hollywood**	22
🗹 Langham Huntington | **Pasadena**	25

🗹 Mastro's Steak | **Beverly Hills**	26
Mixville | **Silver Lake**	25
Musso & Frank | **Hollywood**	23
🗹 Peninsula | **Beverly Hills**	26
🗹 Polo Lounge | **Beverly Hills**	27
Seven Grand | **Downtown**	24
🗹 Shutters | **Santa Monica**	25
Tower Bar | **W Hollywood**	23
Traxx | **Downtown**	21
Windows Lounge | **Beverly Hills**	25

TEQUILA

El Carmen | **Crescent Hts**	20
El Cid | **Silver Lake**	20
La Cita | **Downtown**	19
L Scorpion | **Hollywood**	21
Mayan | **Downtown**	19
Velvet Margarita | **Hollywood**	21

VODKA

Arsenal | **West LA**	19
Bar | **Hollywood**	-
Bar Lubitsch | **W Hollywood**	21
🗹 Bar Marmont | **W Hollywood**	26
Bar Noir | **Beverly Hills**	24
Belmont | **W Hollywood**	19
Bungalow Club | **Melrose**	20
Cameo Bar | **Santa Monica**	25
Chalet | **Eagle Rock**	22
🗹 Chateau Marmont | **W Hollywood**	26
Falcon | **Hollywood**	21
Firefly | **Studio City**	24
Golden Gopher | **Downtown**	22
Guy's | **Crescent Hts**	24
🗹 Hotel Bel-Air | **Bel-Air**	27
King King | **Hollywood**	22
Liquid Kitty | **West LA**	19
🗹 Mastro's Steak | **Beverly Hills**	26
Nic's | **Beverly Hills**	22

Nine Thirty	**Westwood**	23
Polo Lounge	**Beverly Hills**	27
Room	**multi.**	19
Tower Bar	**W Hollywood**	23

WINE BARS

Air Conditioned	**Santa Monica**	19
Bodega Wine	**multi.**	22
BottleRock	**Culver City**	20
NEW Corkbar	**Downtown**	-
Lou	**Hollywood**	23
NEW Must	**Downtown**	-
Otheroom	**Venice**	22
NEW Salute Wine	**Santa Monica**	-
Sgt. Recruiter	**Los Feliz**	-

WINE BY THE GLASS
(See also Wine Bars, above)

Bar Marmont	**W Hollywood**	26
Bar Noir	**Beverly Hills**	24
Belmont	**W Hollywood**	19
Cameo Bar	**Santa Monica**	25
East/West	**W Hollywood**	21
Falcon	**Hollywood**	21
Firefly	**Studio City**	24
Gallery Bar	**Downtown**	-
here	**W Hollywood**	19
Hotel Bel-Air	**Bel-Air**	27
Langham Huntington	**Pasadena**	25
Mastro's Steak	**Beverly Hills**	26
Mixville	**Silver Lake**	25
Moonshadows	**Malibu**	25
Nine Thirty	**Westwood**	23
O-Bar	**W Hollywood**	21
Renee's	**Santa Monica**	20
Shutters	**Santa Monica**	25
Tower Bar	**W Hollywood**	23
Veranda	**Downtown**	-
Vibrato	**Bel-Air**	25

EXPENSE-ACCOUNTERS

NEW ADCB	**W Hollywood**	22
NEW Apple	**W Hollywood**	-
Area	**W Hollywood**	19
Asia de Cuba	**W Hollywood**	24
NEW Bardot	**Hollywood**	21
Bar Marmont	**W Hollywood**	26
Bar NINETEEN12	**Beverly Hills**	23
Bar Noir	**Beverly Hills**	24
Boulevard 3	**Hollywood**	23
Cabana Club	**Hollywood**	20
Cameo Bar	**Santa Monica**	25
Central	**Hollywood**	-
Chateau Marmont	**W Hollywood**	26
Coco de Ville	**W Hollywood**	24
NEW Conga Room	**Downtown**	21
NEW Copa d'Oro	**Santa Monica**	21
NEW Corkbar	**Downtown**	-
Crimson	**Hollywood**	23
NEW Crocker Club	**Downtown**	-
NEW Crown Bar	**W Hollywood**	22
Elevate Lounge	**Downtown**	23
Eleven	**W Hollywood**	21
Foxtail	**W Hollywood**	23
NEW Halo	**Hollywood**	-
Hotel Bel-Air	**Bel-Air**	27
NEW h.wood	**Hollywood**	-
Hyde Lounge	**W Hollywood**	23
Langham Huntington	**Pasadena**	25
LAX	**Hollywood**	21
Les Deux	**Hollywood**	23
Mastro's Steak	**Beverly Hills**	26
Mood	**Hollywood**	20
NEW MyHouse	**Hollywood**	25
Nic's	**Beverly Hills**	22
Nine Thirty	**Westwood**	23

O-Bar	**W Hollywood**	21
Opera	**Hollywood**	23
☑ Peninsula	**Beverly Hills**	26
☑ Polo Lounge	**Beverly Hills**	27
NEW Salute Wine	**Santa Monica**	-
Seven Grand	**Downtown**	24
☑ Shutters	**Santa Monica**	25
☑ Sidebar	**Beverly Hills**	26
☑ Skybar	**W Hollywood**	25
Social H'wood	**Hollywood**	22
Stone Rose	**Crescent Hts**	24
Teddy's	**Hollywood**	24
Tropicana	**Hollywood**	23
Villa	**W Hollywood**	20
Whiskey Blue	**Westwood**	22
Windows Lounge	**Beverly Hills**	25
X Bar	**Century City**	20

FINE FOOD TOO

NEW ADCB	**W Hollywood**	22
☑ Asia de Cuba	**W Hollywood**	24
NEW Barbarella	**Silver Lake**	-
☑ Bar Marmont	**W Hollywood**	26
Bodega Wine	**multi.**	22
BottleRock	**Culver City**	20
Bungalow Club	**Melrose**	20
Chloe	**Santa Monica**	23
NEW Conga Room	**Downtown**	21
NEW Corkbar	**Downtown**	-
NEW Crown Bar	**W Hollywood**	22
NEW Cuba Libre	**Los Feliz**	23
NEW Dakota	**Santa Monica**	22
Eleven	**W Hollywood**	21
Falcon	**Hollywood**	21
Firefly	**Studio City**	24
NEW Kitchen 24	**Hollywood**	-
LAMILL	**Silver Lake**	23
NEW Laurel Tavern	**Studio City**	25
Lou	**Hollywood**	23

L Scorpion	**Hollywood**	21
☑ Mastro's Steak	**Beverly Hills**	26
Medusa	**Silver Lake**	19
Mint	**Mid-City**	21
Musso & Frank	**Hollywood**	23
Nic's	**Beverly Hills**	22
Pete's	**Downtown**	19
☑ Polo Lounge	**Beverly Hills**	27
Rainbow	**W Hollywood**	22
NEW Salute Wine	**Santa Monica**	-
Sgt. Recruiter	**Los Feliz**	-
Social H'wood	**Hollywood**	22
NEW Suede	**Downtown**	-
Traxx	**Downtown**	21
NEW Upper Manhattan	**Manhattan Bch**	23
☑ Vibrato	**Bel-Air**	25
Zinc	**Manhattan Bch**	22

GAMES

DARTS

Casey's	**Downtown**	20
Cat & Fiddle	**Hollywood**	22
Cock 'n Bull	**Santa Monica**	19
Daily Pint	**Santa Monica**	18
Del's Saloon	**West LA**	16
Drawing Room	**Los Feliz**	19
Frank 'n Hank	**Koreatown**	-
Hollywood Billiards	**Hollywood**	19
Joint	**Pico-Robertson**	16
Little Bar	**Mid-Wilshire**	-
McCabe's	**Santa Monica**	18
Molly Malone's	**Fairfax**	19
Power House	**Hollywood**	24
Roost	**Atwater Vill**	19
Roosterfish	**Venice**	18

POOL HALL

Hollywood Billiards	**Hollywood**	19

POOL TABLES
(See also Pool Hall, above)

☒ Barney's Beanery | **W Hollywood**	18
Brig | **Venice**	18
Casey's | **Downtown**	20
Cock 'n Bull | **Santa Monica**	19
Cohiba | **Long Bch**	18
Daily Pint | **Santa Monica**	18
Del's Saloon | **West LA**	16
Ercole's | **Manhattan Bch**	20
Faultline | **Silver Lake**	26
NEW Fifth | **Valley Village**	-
Footsie's | **Highland Pk**	-
Frank 'n Hank | **Koreatown**	-
Fubar | **W Hollywood**	18
Garter | **Venice**	17
Joint | **Pico-Robertson**	16
Little Joy | **Echo Pk**	21
McCabe's | **Santa Monica**	18
Mother Lode | **W Hollywood**	14
NoBAR | **N Hollywood**	20
Normandie | **W Hollywood**	18
Roosterfish | **Venice**	18
Saddle Ranch | **multi.**	18
Seven Grand | **Downtown**	24
Short Stop | **Echo Pk**	18
Social H'wood | **Hollywood**	22
Spaceland | **Silver Lake**	22

VIDEO GAMES

Akbar | **Silver Lake**	19
☒ Barney's Beanery | **W Hollywood**	18
Bar 107 | **Downtown**	21
Del's Saloon | **West LA**	16
Drawing Room | **Los Feliz**	19
Faultline | **Silver Lake**	26
NEW Fifth | **Valley Village**	-
Frank 'n Hank | **Koreatown**	-
Frolic Room | **Hollywood**	22
Fubar | **W Hollywood**	18
Garter | **Venice**	17
Golden Gopher | **Downtown**	22
Happy Ending | **Hollywood**	-
Hollywood Billiards | **Hollywood**	19
Joint | **Pico-Robertson**	16
Little Bar | **Mid-Wilshire**	-
Little Joy | **Echo Pk**	21
Molly Malone's | **Fairfax**	19
Mother Lode | **W Hollywood**	14
Other Side | **Silver Lake**	-
Parlor | **Santa Monica**	20
Power House | **Hollywood**	24
Rainbow | **W Hollywood**	22
Roosterfish | **Venice**	18
Short Stop | **Echo Pk**	18
Silverlake | **Silver Lake**	16
Spaceland | **Silver Lake**	22

GAY
(See also Lesbian;
* certain nights only)

☒ Abbey | **W Hollywood**	23
Akbar | **Silver Lake**	19
Avalon* | **Hollywood**	20
Eagle LA | **Silver Lake**	25
East/West | **W Hollywood**	21
Eleven | **W Hollywood**	21
Faultline | **Silver Lake**	26
Fubar | **W Hollywood**	18
here | **W Hollywood**	19
Library Coffee | **Long Bch**	22
Micky's | **W Hollywood**	-
Mother Lode | **W Hollywood**	14
Oil Can Harry's | **Studio City**	19
Other Side | **Silver Lake**	-
Rage | **W Hollywood**	14
Roosterfish | **Venice**	18
Ultra Suede | **W Hollywood**	18

HOTEL BARS

Bel-Air, Hotel
   🅕 Hotel Bel-Air | **Bel-Air**   27

Beverly Hills Hotel
   Bar NINETEEN12 | 23
   Beverly Hills
   🅕 Polo Lounge | **Beverly Hills** 27

Chateau Marmont
   🅕 Chateau Marmont | 26
   W Hollywood

Figueroa Hotel
   Veranda | **Downtown**   -

Four Seasons Hotel
   Windows Lounge | 25
   Beverly Hills

Hyatt Regency Century Plaza
   X Bar | **Century City**   20

Langham Huntington Hotel
   🅕 Langham Huntington | 25
   Pasadena

Maison 140 Hotel
   Bar Noir | **Beverly Hills**   24

Millennium Biltmore Hotel
   Gallery Bar | **Downtown**   -

Mondrian Hotel
   NEW ADCB | **W Hollywood**   22
   🅕 Asia de Cuba | 24
   W Hollywood
   🅕 Skybar | **W Hollywood**   25

Peninsula Hotel Beverly Hills
   🅕 Peninsula | **Beverly Hills**   26

Regent Beverly Wilshire
   🅕 Sidebar | **Beverly Hills**   26

Roosevelt Hotel
   Teddy's | **Hollywood**   24
   Tropicana | **Hollywood**   23

Shade Hotel
   Zinc | **Manhattan Bch**   22

Shutters on the Beach
   🅕 Shutters | **Santa Monica**   25

Sofitel Los Angeles
   Stone Rose | **Crescent Hts**   24

Standard Hotel
   Standard (Sunset) | 21
   W Hollywood
   🅕 Standard (Downtown) | 25
   Downtown

Sunset Tower Hotel
   Tower Bar | **W Hollywood**   23

Viceroy Santa Monica
   Cameo Bar | **Santa Monica**   25

Westin Bonaventure Hotel
   Bonaventure | **Downtown**   19
   NEW Suede | **Downtown**   -

W Hotel
   🅕 Nine Thirty | **Westwood**   23
   Whiskey Blue | **Westwood**   22

JAZZ CLUBS

Baked Potato | **Studio City**   19
Catalina Jazz | **Hollywood**   22
Grand Star Jazz | **Chinatown**   20
🅕 Polo Lounge | **Beverly Hills**   27
🅕 Vibrato | **Bel-Air**   25

KARAOKE BARS

(Call to check nights,
times and prices)

Brass Monkey | **Koreatown**   20
Cock 'n Bull | **Santa Monica**   19
Del's Saloon | **West LA**   16
Drawing Room | **Los Feliz**   19
Hideout | **Santa Monica**   17
Liquid Kitty | **West LA**   19
Oil Can Harry's | **Studio City**   19
Orchid | **Koreatown**   19

LESBIAN

(* Certain nights only; call ahead)

here* | **W Hollywood**   19
Normandie | **W Hollywood**   18
Ultra Suede* | **W Hollywood**   18

LIVE ENTERTAINMENT

(See also Blues, Comedy Clubs, Jazz Clubs, Karaoke Bars, Piano Bars)

Airliner | varies | **Lincoln Hts** 18
Avalon | rock | **Hollywood** 20
Bar 107 | jazz/rock | **Downtown** 21
Belmont | varies | **W Hollywood** 19
Bordello | rock | **Downtown** 22
Canyon Club | varies | **Agoura Hills** 19
NEW Club Nokia | rock | **Downtown** 23
Cohiba | R&B | **Long Bch** 18
Echo/Echoplex | rock | **Echo Pk** 22
El Cid | varies | **Silver Lake** 20
El Rey Theatre | varies | **Mid-Wilshire** 23
Hal's | jazz | **Venice** 22
Harvelle's | varies | **Santa Monica** 23
Hotel Café | rock | **Hollywood** 25
Joint | alternative/rock | **Pico-Robertson** 16
Jumbo's | exotic dancers | **Hollywood** 21
Key Club | rock | **W Hollywood** 19
King King | varies | **Hollywood** 22
Knitting Factory | varies | **Hollywood** 19
Largo | varies | **W Hollywood** 19
Little Temple | rock | **Silver Lake** 18
Mama Juana's | salsa | **Studio City** -
Mayan | salsa | **Downtown** 19
McCabe's Guitar | varies | **Santa Monica** 23
Molly Malone's | varies | **Fairfax** 19
Pete's | jazz | **Downtown** 19
Rainbow | rock | **W Hollywood** 22
Redwood | rock | **Downtown** 18
Roxy | varies | **W Hollywood** 20
Silverlake | rock | **Silver Lake** 16

Spaceland | alternative/rock | **Silver Lake** 22
Three Clubs | varies | **Hollywood** 19
Troubadour | rock | **W Hollywood** 22
NEW Upper Manhattan | rock | **Manhattan Bch** 23
Viper Room | alternative/rock | **W Hollywood** 19
Whisky A Go-Go | rock | **W Hollywood** 21
Windows Lounge | varies | **Beverly Hills** 25

MATURE CROWDS

NEW ADCB | **W Hollywood** 22
Air Conditioned | **Santa Monica** 19
Bar NINETEEN12 | **Beverly Hills** 23
Bar Noir | **Beverly Hills** 24
Bodega Wine | **multi.** 22
Bordello | **Downtown** 22
Broadway Bar | **Downtown** 21
Bull Pen | **Redondo Bch** 17
Cabana Club | **Hollywood** 20
Cameo Bar | **Santa Monica** 25
Z Chateau Marmont | **W Hollywood** 26
Chloe | **Santa Monica** 23
Cohiba | **Long Bch** 18
NEW Copa d'Oro | **Santa Monica** 21
NEW Corkbar | **Downtown** -
Z Edison Lounge | **Downtown** 26
Elevate Lounge | **Downtown** 23
Eleven | **W Hollywood** 21
Hal's | **Venice** 22
Harvelle's | **Santa Monica** 23
Hideout | **Santa Monica** 17
Z Hotel Bel-Air | **Bel-Air** 27
Z Langham Huntington | **Pasadena** 25
Largo | **W Hollywood** 19

Lou | **Hollywood**	23
Z Mastro's Steak | **Beverly Hills**	26
Match | **N Hollywood**	-
Mint | **Mid-City**	21
Musso & Frank | **Hollywood**	23
NEW Must | **Downtown**	-
Nic's | **Beverly Hills**	22
Z Nine Thirty | **Westwood**	23
Otheroom | **Venice**	22
Other Side | **Silver Lake**	-
Z Peninsula | **Beverly Hills**	26
Z Polo Lounge | **Beverly Hills**	27
Roosterfish | **Venice**	18
NEW Salute Wine | **Santa Monica**	-
Seven Grand | **Downtown**	24
Z Shutters | **Santa Monica**	25
Social H'wood | **Hollywood**	22
Tower Bar | **W Hollywood**	23
Traxx | **Downtown**	21
Z Troubadour | **W Hollywood**	22
NEW Upper Manhattan | **Manhattan Bch**	23
NEW Varnish | **Downtown**	-
Z Vibrato | **Bel-Air**	25
Windows Lounge | **Beverly Hills**	25
X Bar | **Century City**	20
Zinc | **Manhattan Bch**	22

NEWCOMERS

ADCB | **W Hollywood**	22
Apple | **W Hollywood**	-
Z Association | **Downtown**	27
Barbarella | **Silver Lake**	-
Bar Delux | **Hollywood**	19
Bardot | **Hollywood**	21
Club Nokia | **Downtown**	23
Conga Room | **Downtown**	21
Copa d'Oro | **Santa Monica**	21
Corkbar | **Downtown**	-

Crocker Club | **Downtown**	-
Crown Bar | **W Hollywood**	22
Cuba Libre | **Los Feliz**	23
Dakota | **Santa Monica**	22
Ecco | **Hollywood**	19
Fifth | **Valley Village**	-
Halo | **Hollywood**	-
h.wood | **Hollywood**	-
Kitchen 24 | **Hollywood**	-
Lab | **Downtown**	-
Laurel Tavern | **Studio City**	25
Must | **Downtown**	-
MyHouse | **Hollywood**	25
Salute Wine | **Santa Monica**	-
Stinkers | **Silver Lake**	-
Suede | **Downtown**	-
Upper Manhattan | **Manhattan Bch**	23
Varnish | **Downtown**	-

OUTDOOR SPACES

PATIO/TERRACE

Z Abbey | **W Hollywood**	23
Airliner | **Lincoln Hts**	18
Alibi Room | **Culver City**	18
NEW Apple | **W Hollywood**	-
Area | **W Hollywood**	19
Arsenal | **West LA**	19
Z Asia de Cuba | **W Hollywood**	24
Bar | **Hollywood**	-
NEW Barbarella | **Silver Lake**	-
NEW Bar Delux | **Hollywood**	19
NEW Bardot | **Hollywood**	21
Bar Lubitsch | **W Hollywood**	21
Z Bar Marmont | **W Hollywood**	26
Z Barney's Beanery | **W Hollywood**	18
Bar NINETEEN12 | **Beverly Hills**	23
Belmont | **W Hollywood**	19

Boardner's | **Hollywood**	21
Bodega Wine | **Pasadena**	22
Bonaventure | **Downtown**	19
BottleRock | **Culver City**	20
Boulevard 3 | **Hollywood**	23
Broadway Bar | **Downtown**	21
Bungalow Club | **Melrose**	20
Cabana Club | **Hollywood**	20
Cameo Bar | **Santa Monica**	25
Casey's | **Downtown**	20
Cat & Fiddle | **Hollywood**	22
Central | **Hollywood**	-
Z Chateau Marmont | **W Hollywood**	26
NEW Crown Bar | **W Hollywood**	22
NEW Cuba Libre | **Los Feliz**	23
Eagle LA | **Silver Lake**	25
East/West | **W Hollywood**	21
Echo/Echoplex | **Echo Pk**	22
El Cid | **Silver Lake**	20
Elevate Lounge | **Downtown**	23
Falcon | **Hollywood**	21
Z Father's Office | **Culver City**	23
Faultline | **Silver Lake**	26
Firefly | **Studio City**	24
Footsie's | **Highland Pk**	-
Formosa Café | **W Hollywood**	20
Garter | **Venice**	17
Golden Gopher | **Downtown**	22
Gold Room | **Echo Pk**	-
Green Door | **Hollywood**	20
Griffin | **Atwater Vill**	23
Guy's | **Crescent Hts**	24
Gypsy Café | **Westwood**	18
NEW Halo | **Hollywood**	-
here | **W Hollywood**	19
Hideout | **Santa Monica**	17
Hollywood Billiards | **Hollywood**	19
Hollywood Canteen | **Hollywood**	18

Hotel Café | **Hollywood**	25
NEW h.wood | **Hollywood**	-
Hyde Lounge | **W Hollywood**	23
Intelligentsia | **Silver Lake**	21
Jimmy's | **Hollywood**	22
La Cita | **Downtown**	19
Z Langham Huntington | **Pasadena**	25
LAX | **Hollywood**	21
Les Deux | **Hollywood**	23
Library Ale | **Santa Monica**	22
Lucky Baldwins | **Pasadena**	20
Mandrake | **Culver City**	21
Z Mastro's Steak | **Beverly Hills**	26
Micky's | **W Hollywood**	-
Mixville | **Silver Lake**	25
Mood | **Hollywood**	20
Moonshadows | **Malibu**	25
NEW MyHouse | **Hollywood**	25
Nacional | **Hollywood**	20
Nic's | **Beverly Hills**	22
Z Nine Thirty | **Westwood**	23
O-Bar | **W Hollywood**	21
Opera | **Hollywood**	23
Parlor | **Santa Monica**	20
Pete's | **Downtown**	19
Z Polo Lounge | **Beverly Hills**	27
Power House | **Hollywood**	24
Rage | **W Hollywood**	14
Rainbow | **W Hollywood**	22
Renee's | **Santa Monica**	20
Room | **multi.**	19
Roosterfish | **Venice**	18
Saddle Ranch | **multi.**	18
Seven Grand | **Downtown**	24
Z Shutters | **Santa Monica**	25
Silverlake | **Silver Lake**	16
Z Skybar | **W Hollywood**	25
NEW Stinkers | **Silver Lake**	-

SPECIAL APPEALS

Stone Rose | **Crescent Hts**	24
NEW Suede | **Downtown**	-
Sunset Trocadero | **W Hollywood**	20
3rd Stop | **W Hollywood**	21
Tower Bar | **W Hollywood**	23
Traxx | **Downtown**	21
Tropicana | **Hollywood**	23
Vanguard | **Hollywood**	21
Velvet Margarita | **Hollywood**	21
Veranda | **Downtown**	-
Verdugo | **Glassell Pk**	-
Whiskey Blue | **Westwood**	22
Windows Lounge | **Beverly Hills**	25
World Cafe | **Santa Monica**	20
X Bar | **Century City**	20
Ye Rustic Inn | **Los Feliz**	18
Zinc | **Manhattan Bch**	22

ROOFTOP

Cohiba | **Long Bch**	18
Formosa Café | **W Hollywood**	20
Red Lion | **Silver Lake**	22
☑ Standard (Downtown) | **Downtown**	25
Zinc | **Manhattan Bch**	22

SIDEWALK

Insomnia | **Fairfax**	20
LAMILL | **Silver Lake**	23
Library Coffee | **Long Bch**	22

WATERSIDE

Moonshadows | **Malibu**	25
☑ Shutters | **Santa Monica**	25

PIANO BARS

Dresden Room | **Los Feliz**	23
☑ Hotel Bel-Air | **Bel-Air**	27
☑ Langham Huntington | **Pasadena**	25
☑ Mastro's Steak | **Beverly Hills**	26

Other Side | **Silver Lake**	-
☑ Polo Lounge | **Beverly Hills**	27
☑ Shutters | **Santa Monica**	25

PUB GRUB

Arsenal | **West LA**	19
Boardner's | **Hollywood**	21
Bonaventure | **Downtown**	19
Casey's | **Downtown**	20
Cat & Fiddle | **Hollywood**	22
Cock 'n Bull | **Santa Monica**	19
☑ Father's Office | **multi.**	23
NEW Lab | **Downtown**	-
NEW Laurel Tavern | **Studio City**	25
Library Ale | **Santa Monica**	22
Lucky Baldwins | **Pasadena**	20
McCabe's | **Santa Monica**	18
Molly Malone's | **Fairfax**	19
Parlor | **Santa Monica**	20
Redwood | **Downtown**	18
3rd Stop | **W Hollywood**	21
Tom Bergin's | **Fairfax**	22
York | **Highland Pk**	23

QUIET CONVERSATION

Bar NINETEEN12 | **Beverly Hills**	23
Bar Noir | **Beverly Hills**	24
BottleRock | **Culver City**	20
☑ Chateau Marmont | **W Hollywood**	26
Chloe | **Santa Monica**	23
NEW Dakota | **Santa Monica**	22
Good Luck Bar | **Los Feliz**	21
☑ Hotel Bel-Air | **Bel-Air**	27
☑ Langham Huntington | **Pasadena**	25
☑ Mastro's Steak | **Beverly Hills**	26
Match | **N Hollywood**	-
NEW Must | **Downtown**	-

Polo Lounge | **Beverly Hills** 27

Shutters | **Santa Monica** 25

Tower Bar | **W Hollywood** 23

Veranda | **Downtown** -

Whiskey Blue | **Westwood** 22

X Bar | **Century City** 20

ROMANTIC

NEW ADCB | **W Hollywood** 22

NEW Bar Delux | **Hollywood** 19

Bar Marmont | **W Hollywood** 26

Bar Noir | **Beverly Hills** 24

Cameo Bar | **Santa Monica** 25

Chateau Marmont | **W Hollywood** 26

Chloe | **Santa Monica** 23

NEW Copa d'Oro | **Santa Monica** 21

NEW Crocker Club | **Downtown** -

El Cid | **Silver Lake** 20

Firefly | **Studio City** 24

Gallery Bar | **Downtown** -

Green Door | **Hollywood** 20

Hotel Bel-Air | **Bel-Air** 27

Hotel Café | **Hollywood** 25

Langham Huntington | **Pasadena** 25

Les Deux | **Hollywood** 23

Mastro's Steak | **Beverly Hills** 26

Match | **N Hollywood** -

Mixville | **Silver Lake** 25

Moonshadows | **Malibu** 25

Nine Thirty | **Westwood** 23

O-Bar | **W Hollywood** 21

Peninsula | **Beverly Hills** 26

Polo Lounge | **Beverly Hills** 27

Seven Grand | **Downtown** 24

Sgt. Recruiter | **Los Feliz** -

Shutters | **Santa Monica** 25

Skybar | **W Hollywood** 25

Standard (Downtown) | **Downtown** 25

NEW Suede | **Downtown** -

Tower Bar | **W Hollywood** 23

Traxx | **Downtown** 21

NEW Varnish | **Downtown** -

Veranda | **Downtown** -

Vibrato | **Bel-Air** 25

Windows Lounge | **Beverly Hills** 25

X Bar | **Century City** 20

SPORTS BARS

Barney's Beanery | **W Hollywood** 18

Casey's | **Downtown** 20

Cock 'n Bull | **Santa Monica** 19

Del's Saloon | **West LA** 16

Hollywood Billiards | **Hollywood** 19

Parlor | **Santa Monica** 20

Tom Bergin's | **Fairfax** 22

Winstons | **W Hollywood** 20

SUPPER CLUBS

Canyon Club | **Agoura Hills** 19

Catalina Jazz | **Hollywood** 22

El Cid | **Silver Lake** 20

Mama Juana's | **Studio City** -

NEW Upper Manhattan | **Manhattan Bch** 23

Vibrato | **Bel-Air** 25

TRENDY

Abbey | **W Hollywood** 23

NEW ADCB | **W Hollywood** 22

Akbar | **Silver Lake** 19

Alibi Room | **Culver City** 18

NEW Apple | **W Hollywood** -

Area | **W Hollywood** 19

Arsenal | **West LA** 19

☑ Asia de Cuba	**W Hollywood** 24	☑ Edison Lounge	**Downtown** 26
☑ **NEW** Association	**Downtown** 27	Elevate Lounge	**Downtown** 23
Avalon	**Hollywood** 20	Eleven	**W Hollywood** 21
NEW Barbarella	**Silver Lake** -	Falcon	**Hollywood** 21
NEW Bar Delux	**Hollywood** 19	**NEW** Fifth	**Valley Village** -
NEW Bardot	**Hollywood** 21	Firefly	**Studio City** 24
Bar Lubitsch	**W Hollywood** 21	Formosa Café	**W Hollywood** 20
☑ Bar Marmont	**W Hollywood** 26	4100 Bar	**Silver Lake** 21
Bar NINETEEN12	**Beverly Hills** 23	Foxtail	**W Hollywood** 23
Bar 107	**Downtown** 21	Garter	**Venice** 17
Beauty Bar	**Hollywood** 17	Golden Gopher	**Downtown** 22
Belmont	**W Hollywood** 19	Good Luck Bar	**Los Feliz** 21
Bodega Wine	**multi.** 22	Green Door	**Hollywood** 20
Bordello	**Downtown** 22	Griffin	**Atwater Vill** 23
BottleRock	**Culver City** 20	Gypsy Café	**Westwood** 18
Boulevard 3	**Hollywood** 23	**NEW** Halo	**Hollywood** -
Brig	**Venice** 18	Hal's	**Venice** 22
Bungalow Club	**Melrose** 20	here	**W Hollywood** 19
Cabana Club	**Hollywood** 20	Hotel Café	**Hollywood** 25
Cameo Bar	**Santa Monica** 25	**NEW** h.wood	**Hollywood** -
Central	**Hollywood** -	Hyde Lounge	**W Hollywood** 23
Cha Cha Lounge	**Silver Lake** 19	Intelligentsia	**Silver Lake** 21
☑ Chateau Marmont	**W Hollywood** 26	**NEW** Kitchen 24	**Hollywood** -
	NEW Lab	**Downtown** -
Chloe	**Santa Monica** 23	LAMILL	**Silver Lake** 23
Clear	**Studio City** 15	**NEW** Laurel Tavern	**Studio City** 25
Coco de Ville	**W Hollywood** 24	LAX	**Hollywood** 21
NEW Conga Room	**Downtown** 21	Les Deux	**Hollywood** 23
NEW Copa d'Oro	**Santa Monica** 21	L Scorpion	**Hollywood** 21
NEW Corkbar	**Downtown** -	Mandrake	**Culver City** 21
Crimson	**Hollywood** 23	Match	**N Hollywood** -
NEW Crocker Club	**Downtown** -	Micky's	**W Hollywood** -
NEW Crown Bar	**W Hollywood** 22	Mixville	**Silver Lake** 25
NEW Cuba Libre	**Los Feliz** 23	Mood	**Hollywood** 20
NEW Dakota	**Santa Monica** 22	Mountain Bar	**Chinatown** 19
Dime	**Fairfax** 19	**NEW** MyHouse	**Hollywood** 25
Dresden Room	**Los Feliz** 23	Nacional	**Hollywood** 20
East/West	**W Hollywood** 21	☑ Nine Thirty	**Westwood** 23
NEW Ecco	**Hollywood** 19	O-Bar	**W Hollywood** 21

Opera | **Hollywood**	23	Central | **Hollywood**	-
Otheroom | **Venice**	22	Coco de Ville | **W Hollywood**	24
Room | **multi.**	19	Crimson | **Hollywood**	23
Roost | **Atwater Vill**	19	**NEW** Crown Bar | **W Hollywood**	22
NEW Salute Wine | **Santa Monica**	-	Elevate Lounge | **Downtown**	23
Seven Grand | **Downtown**	24	Foxtail | **W Hollywood**	23
Short Stop | **Echo Pk**	18	Green Door | **Hollywood**	20
Side Door | **Manhattan Bch**	23	Guy's | **Crescent Hts**	24
Silverlake | **Silver Lake**	16	**NEW** Halo | **Hollywood**	-
Z Skybar | **W Hollywood**	25	**NEW** h.wood | **Hollywood**	-
Social H'wood | **Hollywood**	22	Hyde Lounge | **W Hollywood**	23
Standard (Sunset) | **W Hollywood**	21	LAX | **Hollywood**	21
Z Standard (Downtown) | **Downtown**	25	Les Deux | **Hollywood**	23
		NEW MyHouse | **Hollywood**	25
Stone Rose | **Crescent Hts**	24	Opera | **Hollywood**	23
Teddy's | **Hollywood**	24	**Z** Skybar | **W Hollywood**	25
Three Clubs | **Hollywood**	19	**Z** Standard (Downtown) | **Downtown**	25
Tropicana | **Hollywood**	23		
Ultra Suede | **W Hollywood**	18	Teddy's | **Hollywood**	24
Vanguard | **Hollywood**	21	Tropicana | **Hollywood**	23
NEW Varnish | **Downtown**	-	Vice | **Hollywood**	-
Velvet Margarita | **Hollywood**	21	Villa | **W Hollywood**	20
Verdugo | **Glassell Pk**	-	Whiskey Blue | **Westwood**	22
Vice | **Hollywood**	-		

SPECIAL APPEALS

Villa | **W Hollywood**	20		
Well | **Hollywood**	19	**VIEWS**	
Winstons | **W Hollywood**	20	**Z** Asia de Cuba | **W Hollywood**	24
Woods | **Hollywood**	20	Bar NINETEEN12 | **Beverly Hills**	23
X Bar | **Century City**	20	Bonaventure | **Downtown**	19
York | **Highland Pk**	23	Cohiba | **Long Bch**	18
Zanzibar | **Santa Monica**	20	Elevate Lounge | **Downtown**	23
Zinc | **Manhattan Bch**	22	**Z** Langham Huntington | **Pasadena**	25

VELVET ROPE

		Moonshadows | **Malibu**	25
NEW Apple | **W Hollywood**	-	**Z** Shutters | **Santa Monica**	25
Area | **W Hollywood**	19	**Z** Skybar | **W Hollywood**	25
NEW Bar Delux | **Hollywood**	19	Standard (Sunset) | **W Hollywood**	21
NEW Bardot | **Hollywood**	21	**Z** Standard (Downtown) | **Downtown**	25
Cabana Club | **Hollywood**	20	Tower Bar | **W Hollywood**	23

Wine Vintage Chart

This chart (prepared by University of South Carolina law professor **Howard Stravitz,** and based on our 0 to 30 ratings scale) reflects the vintage quality and the wine's readiness to drink.

Whites

	89	90	94	95	96	97	98	99	00	01	02	03	04	05	06	07
French:																
Alsace	24	25	24	23	23	22	25	23	25	26	22	21	24	25	24	-
Burgundy	23	22	-	27	26	23	21	25	25	24	27	23	26	27	25	23
Loire Valley	-	-	-	-	-	-	-	-	24	25	26	22	23	27	24	-
California:																
Chardonnay	-	-	-	-	-	-	24	23	26	26	25	26	29	25	-	
Sauvignon Blanc	-	-	-	-	-	-	-	-	-	-	-	26	27	26	27	26
German:	26	27	24	23	26	25	26	23	21	29	27	24	26	28	24	-

Reds

	89	90	94	95	96	97	98	99	00	01	02	03	04	05	86	88
French:																
Bordeaux	25	29	21	26	25	23	25	24	29	26	24	26	24	28	25	23
Burgundy	24	26	-	26	27	25	22	27	22	24	27	25	24	27	25	-
Rhône	28	28	23	26	22	24	27	26	27	26	-	26	24	27	25	-
California:																
Cab./Merlot	-	28	29	27	25	28	23	26	-	27	26	25	24	26	23	-
Pinot Noir	-	-	-	-	-	-	-	24	23	25	28	26	27	25	24	-
Zinfandel	-	-	-	-	-	-	-	-	-	25	23	27	22	23	23	-
Oregon:																
Pinot Noir	-	-	-	-	-	-	-	-	-	-	27	25	26	27	26	-
Italian:																
Tuscany	-	25	23	24	20	29	24	27	24	27	-	25	27	25	24	-
Piedmont	27	27	-	-	26	27	26	25	28	27	-	24	23	26	25	24
Spanish:																
Rioja	-	-	26	26	24	25	-	25	24	27	-	24	25	26	24	-
Australian:																
Shiraz/Cab.	-	-	24	26	23	26	28	24	24	27	27	25	26	26	24	-